Dis

Message from the author

*"This is an opinions-based book; it is not intended as binding legal,
financial or compliance advice. However, I have made every effort
to offer perspectives and opinions that are current and unbiased.
These opinions are my own, and I do not suggest that contributors,
sponsors, former colleagues or previous employers endorse or
share those opinions."*

Meet The Author

Heather began working in the food service industry in 2000. Since then, she has worked in eight countries and over 1000 food service businesses. Trained in the UK as an environmental health practitioner, she has specialised in food safety, working with companies, The Olympic Games and the world's largest chain restaurant brands. In recent years, her focus has turned to dietary needs and preferences, helping companies move beyond basic compliance and into customer service, marketing and branding.

Why? Heather is uniquely able to connect the dots within the industry and bring together experts to find solutions. Personally, she has dealt with food allergies and struggled to find options suitable for her vegan diet. Professionally, she has travelled the world helping restaurants and hotels keep to food safety and brand standards. With her up-close view, she's witnessed both the weaknesses in the food service industry and the best of the best.

Heather is passionate about a win-win scenario where people feel included when they eat out and food service businesses are successful.

Dedication

First, to the readers: the many individuals in the food service industry. I have written this book for you. Thank you for being curious and opening it. I hope it serves you well and that the post-pandemic world is kind to you. For those who prefer to listen or like to learn virtually, I have produced an overview of this book in a short online course. The course is complimentary with this book, and you can invite anyone interested.

ultimatestarter.heatherlandex.com

I also dedicate this book to all my contributors, beta readers, previous employers, colleagues, associates and clients who enriched me with the experiences, learning opportunities and collective expertise needed to write this book. You have helped make me the person I am today.

Finally, this book is dedicated to my husband Alex, who made it possible in so many ways. Thank you for having my back, for giving me courage and for introducing me to the vegetarian lifestyle so many years ago. You are and have always been my soulmate and an absolute sweetheart.

Foreword by Gerry Robert
international bestselling author of
Millionaire Mindset

Heather has bravely exposed the perspectives of two relatively unknown worlds in order to assist food service businesses in seeing opportunities that already exist: **the money left on the table.**

Inspiring people to care more and act in kindness is no simple feat. When I first heard Heather's concept of serving more people to earn more profits, the logic seemed too simple. Inclusivity is a philosophy that can be applied universally, across different food businesses, across borders and across cultures. It is refreshing to see someone so passionate, putting experts together and synthesizing their input in an entertaining, uniquely charismatic and relatable book.

The food service industry is a fundamental necessity of modern-day life. Heather's insight and the collected contributions from industry experts could impact millions of lives by reducing risk and increasing the benefits to both customers and food industry professionals.

I started my own entrepreneurial journey following a seminar about mindset. The power of perspective is incredible. Heather's perspective—which joins knowledge in the areas of compliance, marketing innovation and food safety in order to attract overlooked minority groups—is **genius**. Fundamentally, Heather's book encourages a mindset shift that will grow businesses and boost customer satisfaction into the future.

Heather's book has potential to impact the world, challenge the status quo and above all, help people be nicer to one another.

Reading her book is a safe, low-cost investment that will get you on your way towards inclusivity. All you have to do is be open to a new perspective. Simple.

Foreword by Korie Minkus
CEO of Industry Rockstar, founder of Rock Your Product and business mentor

Heather is a master at connecting knowledge to strengthen the reach and impact of everyday businesses. She is not afraid of what's in front of her; she is fully committed to prioritising both healthy outcomes for her client partners and sustainable brand market share growth.

Having the opportunity to work with Heather adds a layer of warmth to any business endeavour. Heather's intuitive genius in connecting talent in the food service industry and the consumers' growing demand for dietary options is illuminating and altering businesses around the planet. Heather's voice is one of answers, of solutions and options, because she is powerfully committed to successful outcomes.

"The goal of this book is to help you create uncontested market space and make the competition irrelevant."

from **_Multiply Your Business_**
by Gerry Robert

Contents

Where this story starts

In August 2019, I was taken by ambulance to the hospital emergency room for suspected anaphylaxis, a life-threatening allergic reaction. I had never experienced anything like it.

I had spent the previous night in a hotel, which I often did at that time. I was traveling a lot, working on behalf of one of the world's largest compliance companies to audit international chain restaurants for their brand and food safety standards.

Nothing out of the ordinary.

Except I had woken up that day feeling tingly. My lips and eyes were also a bit puffy, and a rash had started to appear on my chest. I had a few urgent bathroom visits, but nothing seemed especially alarming. I was tired, I thought, from travelling long hours the day before. Perhaps there was a bit too much perfume in the hotel soap or laundry. I had been a bit warm during the night—maybe it was heat rash.

I had plenty of possible explanations, but when I rang the national emergency medical hotline for advice (it was early morning), the nurse suggested I go to hospital. That seemed like an overreaction, so instead I took a cold shower, went to breakfast and planned to buy antihistamines when the pharmacy opened.

By the time I got to breakfast, my lips had swelled up a bit more. More worryingly, they started feeling numb. I told the receptionist at checkout that I was feeling funny, and she offered me an antihistamine. I took one and said I would sit somewhere she could see me in case I got worse. I assumed I'd be better within half an hour.

I had a coffee and did a bit of work in reception. Suddenly, I felt like I would pass out, even though I was sitting down. My hands and nails had gone bone white and completely numb, and my feet were also numb. I felt wheezy, and I struggled to walk over to the reception desk. I could not even hold my head up or inhale deeply enough to say the word "ambulance".

The receptionist asked me to lie down behind the reception with my legs raised. The ambulance arrived quickly, but by the time I was safely loaded and they had begun monitoring my vital signs, the rash had spread all the way down my torso to my belly button. The paramedic did an exceptionally good job of calming me down, but, as a food safety trainer and friend of allergy sufferers, I know the symptoms of anaphylactic shock.

Did you know that one of the lesser-known symptoms of a severe allergy attack is the feeling of impending doom? I definitely experienced that. I texted my husband a final goodbye and "I love you". He was a plane flight away with two small kids, no childcare and no ability to get to me—I was terrified.

At the hospital, I was given immunosuppressants and strong antihistamines. Staff also completed an ECG (electrocardiogram) and blood tests. The doctor confirmed a severe allergic reaction and sent me on my way with some hardcore pills to get me home safely. I didn't make it to work that day and continued to feel shaky, but the doctor had said I could fly. On the flight home I developed a tremor in my arms and hives on my face and neck, which was... concerning.

The point in telling you this story is that I didn't eat anything out of the home for a couple of weeks. I was completely anxious about eating at all.

I was scared I could die.

The doctor had mentioned a milk allergy, which had never been suggested to me before. I was vegan by then, but I had noticed several incidences where I'd had symptoms similar to food poisoning after eating at hotel breakfast buffets. Being well-versed in food safety, I knew "traces" of milk are in nearly everything, so it seemed like a reasonable possibility. Eventually, however, after some delays and a round of lost test results, my doctor ruled out a milk allergy and referred me to an allergist for further testing. The earliest appointment was four months later.

This experience showed me the perspectives of real-life food allergy sufferers. I understood first-hand how it felt to live in fear, scared to eat—especially to eat out, including at work, school, conferences, trainings and public events. Having a severe food allergy affected every part of my life, because food is such an important aspect of our social, work and educational environments, not to mention everyday life.

My own path to diagnosis has so far been somewhat inconclusive. I did discover that, like many other vegans, I had unknowingly become lactose intolerant—severely so, in my case. I also have severe dust mite and grass allergies, but it is unclear whether those issues were responsible for the severe allergic reaction I experienced that day. Stress, tiredness or dehydration may have made my reaction worse. Or I might have a mild allergy to certain fruits, shellfish, nightshades...anything!

The immune system and causes of allergy are complex. It's often not sorted out by a blood test or skin prick test, and reactions can be the result of multiple factors or multiple allergies. **Allergies are individual, variable, difficult to treat and rarely curable.**

Since this rather traumatic event, I have noticed how prevalent allergies are. Moreover, statistics consistently indicate the number of people with allergies is increasing.

I have also observed first-hand the challenges—and dangers—that exist for allergy sufferers in the food service industry. First and foremost is a lack of awareness, both on the part of food service professionals and on the part of the allergy sufferer. Some food service staff may label allergy sufferers "picky eaters", misunderstanding or dismissing the best practices needed to keep them safe. Meanwhile, allergy sufferers may be ignorant to what goes on in a commercial kitchen, or they may not know the ins and outs of food labelling disclaimers. This lack of awareness creates risk for both the business and the customer.

And this is where my personal life merged with my professional life. I knew I was uniquely positioned because of my food safety compliance expertise combined with my personal experiences as someone with specific dietary needs.

I had to write this book.

*If you yourself have an allergy, download the Teal App from the QR code at the back of this book in **Author Resources.***

There is more on my story in
bonuschapter.heatherlandex.com

"

Every individual matters and deserves to be served food which is safe for them to eat, and to be treated with respect for their beliefs, needs and choices.

The segment of the market consisting of those with specific dietary needs and preferences is big and fast-growing.

We live in a changing world. This book aims to help you embrace, not fear, this diversity.

-Heather Landex

Part 1

Inclusivity in Food Service:

The Business Perspective

Everyone has to be able to eat.
This simple statement is both a challenge and a business opportunity.

During my years in the food service industry, both in my humble beginnings as food service staff and in my later experiences as an Environmental Health Practitioner/Food Safety Auditor/ Safety Advisor and Environmental Health Consultant, I have seen many ways in which businesses are not meeting the needs of their increasingly diverse customer base. The goal of this book is to *inspire and encourage the industry to prioritize their food safety standards, improving their overall level of service by becoming more inclusive to people with dietary needs and preferences.* I hope to motivate a change in mindset that can help businesses look to the future as they navigate the post-pandemic recovery.

🍂 My advice and opinions may challenge your perspective and shake the status quo because my goal is to help you *recognize the money left on the table* when businesses only cater to so-called "typical eaters".

I want to help the industry be better at ***inclusivity*, the conscious development and implementation of practices and/or policies that include people who might otherwise be excluded or marginalized.**

Inclusivity doesn't just benefit the consumer. It's a way to increase the number of customers you are able to serve. It also increases customer loyalty and generates organic marketing opportunities.

The goal of *inclusivity* benefits restaurants, takeaways, caterers, hotels, cafes, coffee shops, bakeries, kiosks, delis, conferencing facilities, workplaces, care facilities and hospitals, charities, events, entertainment venues, educational institutions, museums, tourist attractions, bars, nightclubs, street food stalls, markets, sandwich shops, mobile vendors—anywhere and everywhere food is served to the end consumer. It even has benefits for food manufacturers.

It doesn't matter what your job role is. The whole hierarchy of the industry—CEOs and owners, chefs and servers, customer service and marketing staff, everyone!—should all be focused on better understanding their customers...and the customer's decision-making process.

The world is changing...

...and it's changing faster than ever. Take, for example:
- Increase in consumer demand for plant-based products
- Rise in vegan and vegetarian diets
- Increase in the prevalence of food allergies
- Environmental crises driving the interest in and importance of sustainability
- Increased incidence of diabetes, obesity, heart disease, cancers (often linked to diet)
- Increased importance of hygiene in a post-pandemic world

Why are these relevant trends? They affect the way people eat, and they are influencing behaviours, particularly consumers' buying behaviours and how they eat out.

What it also means: Several market sectors are waiting to be served or served better. I am going to show you how to cut a piece of that pie. I am not suggesting you should become a vegan restaurant—leave that to the vegans. But if you already run a vegan restaurant? Your business can still learn how to be more inclusive.

Change is hard, but often rewarding.

I aim to show you ways to make it easier for yourself, without changing your concept, should you decide to shift how you do things.

This book is not all about vegans or allergy sufferers or any other specific subset of the consumer. Nor is it all about compliance, though it may feel like each of those things at different points. *This book is about giving food businesses a competitive edge.*

By the end of this book, you should be able to decide:

Are you in or are you out?

Inclusivity requires a definitive decision and a real, top-down commitment. Half-doing it, pretending to do it or exaggerating your capabilities of doing it will backfire, endangering your customers and your brand. After reading this book, you are completely entitled to return to business as usual, simply a little wiser or more aware. But at the very least, my hope is that this book helps you to relate to your customers better. That's always positive in business.

You may also discover a short way of explaining complex matters to others, enabling your staff to increase service efficiency and—most importantly—safety. When you increase safety and build systems to reduce mistakes, you create an excellent customer experience while you also reduce complaints, liability and risk to reputation.

I have visited hundreds and thousands of food service outlets, both as a consumer and as a professional. I observe the good, the bad and the **GENIUS**. The injustices I see are:

● Small businesses are too afraid to attempt mastering the legislation, as it appears too complex.

● The larger chains with their internal compliance teams are either too scared of litigation, or their high volume inhibits their ability to adapt and include more people.

These two problems leave a lot of people with specific dietary preferences excluded.

Many of the more than fifty individuals I interviewed for this book said that the industry as a whole "doesn't care" about these minorities. In these pages, I'm going to show you *why you should care.*

> **José Luis Cabañero, Spain—founder and CEO at Eatable Adventures, a global food innovation hub**
> *"There is a market need, but restaurant owners don't totally re-alise the potential. Regulations [for food allergy management] aren't clear. You don't really need special equipment or rooms for the majority of clients; you just need to be mindful and have proper procedures for cleaning, preparation and ingredient separation. There's not a need for hospital-grade cleanliness in order to produce gluten-free food. You can have gluten-free items and not be a fully gluten-free restaurant. I eat gluten-free myself, and I can safely eat at many places that aren't totally gluten-free. But restaurants don't really have the mentality to adopt gluten-free as part of their offering."*

> **Richard Ebbs, UK—director of commercial and marketing at Synergy Grill, a catering equipment manufacturing company**
> *"I have six kids. Four of them are vegan and another is vege-*

tarian, as is my wife. It's a growing trend which is not going away.... The entire food service industry, starting with the manufacturers of equipment down to the chefs, have to meet customer needs. Otherwise, customers will eat elsewhere."

Free Resources

You can find links to articles, statistics, campaigns and other free resources at **freeresources.heatherlandex.com**

Chapter 1

What Is Inclusivity?

In this chapter:
The inclusivity pyramid
Current barriers to inclusivity

There are almost limitless dietary preferences. Covering each individual possibility is outside the scope of this book. Instead, this book aims to provide key concepts and best practices focused on the foundations of inclusivity.

Above all, I spoke with individuals throughout the industry to gather their perspectives and ***construct a holistic view of the opportunity for inclusivity***…including how well-executed inclusivity can establish a food service provider as more exclusive and prestigious.

1.1 The Inclusivity Pyramid
Imagine inclusivity as a pyramid, with basic compliance at the base (the low bar) and inclusivity at the peak (achieved by few).

This concept is discussed in depth in Part 3, but the basic principles are simple:

Basic Compliance – All food businesses are expected to meet basic compliance requirements, which are the country-specific legal minimum requirements for food safety. For example, separation of raw and cooked ingredients.

Food Safety Standards – To protect their brand reputation, many food businesses have implemented food safety standards above the legal minimum requirements. This is particularly true of franchises and chain food service providers. However, a good food safety culture—though valuable—doesn't address the inclusion of people with dietary preferences.

Allergy Management – Most food businesses stop at allergy awareness. Not many have the robust allergy management practices needed to consistently and safely serve people who have food allergies or intolerances. Therefore, strong allergy management is a *unique selling point (USP)* that sets a business apart as exclusive.

Inclusivity – With both a robust food safety culture and capable allergy management in place, a small minority of food service businesses serve people with dietary preferences *really well*. Inclusive businesses actively welcome and serve diners of all kinds, communicate with them exceptionally well and offer a variety of choices that take dietary preferences into account, whether those are a result of *allergies or choice*.

Successful inclusivity depends on having the lower tiers of the pyramid in place first; that is, basic compliance, a strong food safety culture and robust allergy management.

1.2 Current barriers to inclusivity

Being more inclusive makes a business more exclusive. Because inclusivity demonstrates professionalism, competence and quality, it confers prestige. Additionally, inclusivity creates brand-loyal customers and, via USPs, marketing opportunities.

What are the challenges that keep many food service businesses at the bottom of that pyramid?

Some particularly modern-day risks are:

- **Contamination** of plant-based and vegan products with animal products (Milk and egg are the most common allergies, and milk is responsible for most of the fatal anaphylactic allergic reactions in the UK.)
- **Lack of allergy awareness** and control, particularly in restaurant kitchens, including the widely varying use of "may contain" disclaimers
- **Vague training requirements** for food handlers

Example

As someone with severe lactose intolerance who often has to travel for work, I often get sick with food-poisoning-like symptoms from eating outside my home. Each time, I am surprised, because I stay and eat at reputable places and am typically served by kind and attentive staff. But prevention of milk contamination is one thing these businesses don't do very well, and that problem is systemic, widespread and persistent. In my case, small traces of milk have big consequences. Not only am I frequently ill, but I legally cannot do my job. Any sign of a potentially food-borne illness restricts me from making site visits.

However, that same professional background has helped me see what many other customers in my situation may not have seen or been in a position to do anything about: exceptional food safety systems and training can set a business apart.

Takeaways
- Inclusivity is built on a foundation of consistent food safety standards, food safety culture and allergy management practices.
- Relatively few businesses are competing in the inclusive market space. Exceptional food safety systems and training can make your business prestigious.
- Being inclusive is the new exclusive.

Chapter 2

Dietary Preferences

In this chapter:
What is a dietary preference?
What does inclusive look like?
Who is currently excluded?
The market opportunity

2.1 What is a dietary preference?

In the context of this book, a *dietary preference* refers to any decision to eat in a way which the industry considers atypical.

Although this section might be more accurately called "Dietary Restrictions, Needs and Preferences, and the Growing Market for Them", that's quite a mouthful. More importantly, there is a huge overlap between compulsory and optional dietary restrictions. **You will often not know whether a customer's dietary preference is compulsory or optional (e.g., allergy or choice),** and, as you will see throughout the course of this book, it should not matter. **Regardless of what preferences a customer expresses, your responsibilities remain the same:**

🍃 to listen to and ensure you understand what the customer is asking for

🍃 to know and disclose what's in your products

🍃 to know, explain and uphold robust procedures to prevent contamination with, e.g., allergens[1] and

---

1   *Allergens are the triggers for allergies. From a science perspective, allergens are ordinarily harmless substances that, in some individuals, cause an atypical immune response. More information in Chapter 8.*

◗ to be honest about your ability to safely serve the customer. Usually, dietary preferences involve the avoidance of ingredients and are therefore sometimes called dietary restrictions. However, they can also include the specific methods by which food is prepared or processed, as seen in **halal** (Islamic) and **kosher** (Jewish) diets, among others.

Everyone has their own food likes and dislikes, but food choices motivated by health issues and belief systems affect more absolutely who can and cannot eat from your menu (for the sake of their own personal safety or well-being). If your menu does not recognize and actively include them, those individuals will have to eat elsewhere or not eat.

2.2 What does inclusive look like?

Everyone has to be able to eat. In general terms, inclusivity in food service actively considers people with various dietary preferences and creates options they can eat. These individuals should enjoy their customer experience as much as the industry's "typical" eaters do.

If you are 100% inclusive, you can serve anyone and everyone. Practically speaking, however, it's impossible to plan and prepare for every possible scenario in the incredibly diverse human landscape. Some needs and preferences may be so rare or specialized as to be beyond the capabilities of most chefs or the practicalities of most food establishments.

However, aiming to become *more inclusive* is a low bar that does not offer much of a competitive edge. What, then, is an achievable goal that will yield results?

Be as inclusive as possible, given your resources and circumstances. The goal? To increase your capacity and capabilities in the long term.

2.3 The market opportunity: Who is currently excluded and why?

Key statistics

🍴 Around 60% of allergy sufferers and people with intolerances currently avoid eating out (FSA)

🍴 Lactose intolerance affects 65% of the world population and 10% of Northern Europeans (World Population Review).

🍴 A full 23% of people in the UK are not able to consume milk (Statista, 2018).

🍴 Gluten intolerance (also known as gluten sensitivity) affects around 6% of the population (Beyond Celiac).

🍴 Approximately 1% of the population has coeliac disease, an autoimmune disease triggered by ingesting gluten.

🍴 Conference and event managers report that around 15% of people report a dietary restriction. However, the actual number is likely higher, since some people will either fail to give advance notice or not want to seem "difficult".

Businesses may worry about their ability to safely serve these customers, particularly in the case of those with severe allergies. But businesses that make little to no attempt to be more inclusive are missing out on or losing customers. Let's take a closer look at those often being excluded.

1: Those on the plant-based continuum: The vegans, vegetarians, pescatarians, meat-reducers/reducetarians and Meat-free Monday or Veganuary (vegan January) supporters. How many people is that? Most estimates place vegans at 1–3% of the population and vegetarians at 5–30% of the population, depending on the community. **However, the number of those who are reducing their meat consumption (intentionally or unintentionally) is estimated to be 55% of the population** (in the UK; Agriculture and Horticulture Development Board, November 2020).

2: Those with certain religious beliefs: Globally, more people are religious than aren't. Different religions forbid or discourage pork, beef, shellfish, animal products generally and/or alcohol, either all the time or at certain times of the year. Many religious diets fall somewhere on the plant-based continuum, whether vegan or vegetarian or in between. Religiously motivated diets may require fasting periods, specific restrictions for religious holidays, separation of food during preparation, or certified slaughter methods (e.g., halal or kosher).

3: Those with allergies: (1–10% of the population) Of the at least 170 known food allergens, fourteen are required to be labelled in the EU (eight in the US). The EU-mandated fourteen are milk, egg, crustaceans, molluscs, fish, nuts, peanuts, cereals containing gluten, soya, lupin, celery, sulphur dioxide/sulphites, mustard and sesame.

4: Those with food intolerances: (15–20% of the population) Intolerances are not the same as food allergies but can still be debilitating. Symptoms and effects are discussed in detail in Chapters 6–8.

5: Those with temporary or chronic health conditions: (*Disclaimer: I am not a medical doctor or dietician.*) Individuals may choose or be advised to adopt specific diets as part of managing health conditions including but not limited to: pregnancy, breastfeeding, coeliac disease, Crohns/IBS, diabetes, colitis, heart disease, high blood pressure, high cholesterol and kidney problems.

6: Those with food aversions: Some individuals experience an extreme sensitivity to the smell, texture or taste of certain foods. Any food might cause the reaction, and the revulsion may be individual or cultural. Such food aversions may make an individual physically ill, but any physical symptoms are psychologically driven.

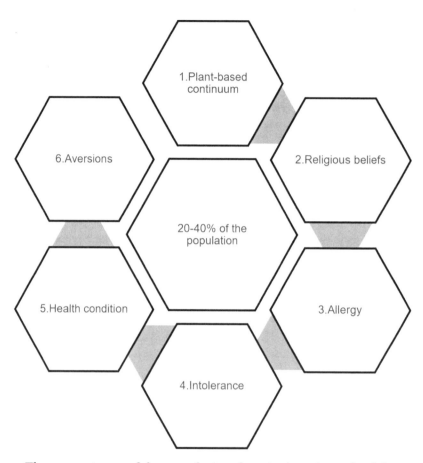

The percentages of the population that stack up in each of the six categories overlap, but I estimate conservatively that anywhere from 20% to approximately 40% of the population have some form of dietary preference. I have rounded down averages for each of the categories.

Even more importantly: **You may not know what—or more specifically, whom—you are missing.** Busy service staff probably do not record every time someone asks for an option which is not available. And often, the customer never even gets as far as making that request; they look at the menu online or in the window, see that there is little to nothing obviously appropriate for them and go elsewhere without a trace.

They may never set foot inside your business.

Takeaways

🍂 The untapped market of those with dietary preferences is likely much bigger than it is commonly believed to be.

🍂 People with dietary preferences are often excluded due to liability concerns (around allergy labelling) and/or lack of awareness.

Free Resources

You can find links to articles, statistics, campaigns and other free resources at **freeresources.heatherlandex.com**

Chapter 3

The Common Denominator Effect

In this chapter:
What is the Common Denominator Effect?
The importance of communication

3.1 What is the Common Denominator Effect?

Eating is a social activity, and people with different diets often find themselves out in a group, trying to choose where to eat. Because ***everyone needs to be able to eat confidently and safely,*** the person with the most restrictive or specialized diet in a group is often the person at the centre of decision-making. That person determines the minimum requirement of the group, or, as I call it, the group's **Common Denominator.**

Take as an example the vegan in the centre of the diagram above. That person will recommend a place where they trust they can eat confidently, and they will take the party with them. Sometimes, it's the people around the vegan who make the actual decision, but they do so to include that person's dietary preferences. In the case of children with allergies or coeliac disease, for example, parents will choose a place where their child can eat. If your business excludes the Common Denominator—either by not having options available or by not clearly communicating those options—you are missing out on the entire group. That isn't just a single lost booking, either. It's a loss that carries into the future due to missed returning trade and profits.

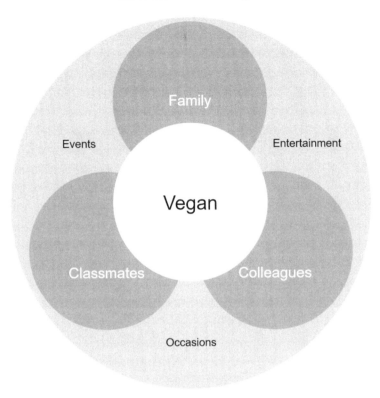

Millie Hall, UK—approved mental health professional (AMPH) and ethical vegan

"If we go out for work, I'm lucky that my managers are very caring and supportive. They will make sure that wherever we decide to go is prepared to do a vegan option.

The places that we go quite often will make a vegan meal especially for me. And they're really good. Don't get me wrong. I've never had a bad one, but I've said to them afterwards, "That was a really, really amazing meal. Why don't you just have it on your menu all the time?" They just didn't get it.

If they hadn't made the meal for me, they would have lost a booking which was over £200. It's not just losing one person— it's losing a booking."

I know several people with dietary preferences who have not attended Christmas parties, weddings, events, workshops or birthday meals because they couldn't eat anything on the menu, not even if they rang ahead.

Event tickets are particularly susceptible to the Common Denominator Effect. When a participant cannot eat the food included at an event or function, the ticket is perceived as overpriced or unfair, especially if participants are not offered a token discount or allowed to bring their own food. I feel the same way when I stay in a hotel which includes breakfast, and I find myself limited to an apple or a gluten-free cracker because everything else contains milk, egg or another animal product. That's why, these days, I make all my reservations at a particular hotel chain that consistently offers a plant-based fridge at breakfast. I am always guaranteed a white coffee and some cereal in the morning. It gives me great comfort to know I can eat an effortless, filling breakfast before starting work or enjoying my vacation.

> **Richard Ebbs, UK—director of commercial and marketing at Synergy Grill, a catering equipment manufacturing company**
> *"The vegans in our family determine where we are going to go to eat. If it doesn't have a good vegan menu, we are not going to go.... The meat eaters will happily eat vegan food, but the vegans won't ever eat meat. So we end up going to vegan-friendly places.*
>
> *From a restauranteur point of view, make sure you are meeting the needs of all your customers. Although you may think it's only 5–10% of your customers that eat vegan, it's also all those "hanger-on-ers", the meat eaters with the vegan, that you're missing.*
>
> *Once CEOs realise how much money they are losing...they will put things in place, and the chefs will follow."*

The Common Denominator Effect doesn't mean that the dining choice is everyone's first option. It does mean that there is a reasonable and substantial menu item or modification option for each person in the group. A salad and chips as the vegan option isn't going to cut it.

This is an opportunity to stand out against the competition!

Yes, allergy sufferers and vegans (to name two commonly excluded groups) are minorities, but serving them effectively will soon stack up in your more typical customer purchases as well. Watch your total sales, not just the sales of inclusive options such as the vegan or allergy-friendly items.

You can bring even more revenue your way by working inclusivity into all areas of the menu. For example, if not everyone can have a coffee because your business doesn't offer a plant-based milk option, or the most decadent gluten-free dessert you offer is a fruit salad, you may miss out on upselling to the whole group.

I am always upset if I miss out on dessert or coffee, so much so that I carry my own (expensive, inconvenient) mini oat milk supply with me to functions and events so that I can participate in the custom of networking with a warm drink. I did the same whilst pregnant, with decaffeinated coffee and non-alcoholic champagne at networking events and a couple of weddings. I would have been thrilled if I had been able to order off the menu instead!

> **CEO of an international pizza chain (anonymous)**
> *"Big corporations—this isn't going to sound good—don't do it because they care about the vegan. We care about losing the people with the vegan. This tiny 1% of products for vegans are to capture the people with the vegan."*

The term "inclusivity" also refers to religiously motivated diets, and the Network Effect also applies to religious groups. And to community groups in general. People talk, and they want to find the places that can meet their needs.

The fantastic thing about inclusivity is that what works to attract one group can often serve another as well. Imagine a café decides to add a naturally sweetened, no-sugar-added whole foods plant-based "cheesecake" to the menu for their vegan customers. That dessert might wind up with a loyal following that also includes diabetics, low-carb and paleo dieters, coeliacs, those with lactose intolerance or a milk allergy, and even your existing customer base. An ideal inclusive menu option can meet the needs of several different groups—more on that in Chapter 11.

Yes, the majority of orders from any one table will still likely be for your standard menu items. The main business benefit of the inclusive option is that typically excluded individuals are happy to visit and buy with *you,* because they can't get the same options and service elsewhere. And if they're excited about you, they will steer their group back to you again and again in the future.

3.2 Communication matters

Perhaps surprisingly, some businesses who already have inclusive options are also leaving money on the table because they aren't effectively communicating what they offer.

Communication is key. That includes **communication with the customer, in marketing efforts** and **within the business**.

Example

I once asked the server in my local bakery what the vegan options were, only to be told that there were zero vegan breads in the entire bakery...in a tone that I heard as, "Thank you, now please leave." When I contacted the managing director, however, it turned out that *all* their breads were vegan, except one (which had cheese). In other words, the options were even *better* than I had thought! Unfortunately, by then my business had moved to the competitor across the road.

In this scenario, all the bakery needed was better training for their staff and either clear labelling or a tiny sign that said "naturally vegan" next to the appropriate options.

Good communication about inclusivity can give the needed edge in a crowded market.

People often have to go places where the food options are set and limited. Think airports, train stations, workplaces, schools, events, hotels and functions. In those environments, having an inclusive menu could be the one thing that helps you stand out against the competition by being *the only inclusive option*.

When I have been delayed at the airport, I have often had no option beyond a packet of crisps. If there'd been any restaurant or shop with a sign advertising a substantial vegan dish, you can bet they would have gotten my business—not just then, but every time I went through that airport.

Takeaways

- Stand out, don't miss out, by including people with dietary preferences. It matters more than you think.
- The Common Denominator Effect means you cannot only watch the sales of inclusive menu options.
- Communication counts!

Free Resources

You can find links to articles, statistics, campaigns and other free resources at **freeresources.heatherlandex.com**

Chapter 4

Exclusivity and the Network Effect

In this chapter:
The Network Effect
How inclusivity leads to exclusivity (prestige)
How to spread the word

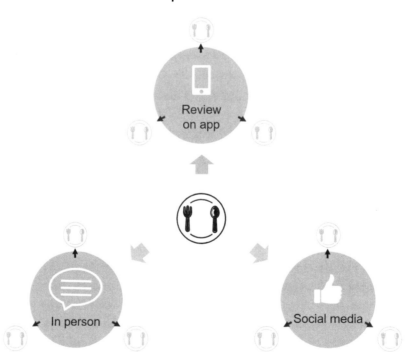

The Network Effect demonstrates the impact one Common Denominator has on their network. The plates with knives and forks represent Common Denominators. The grey circles are networks such as social media, in-person groups, or apps and review sites.

4.1 What is the Network Effect?

We've already seen how people with dietary preferences steer their social groups when choosing to eat out, so you will earn more revenue than just the one inclusive meal. Your business' ability to serve an inclusive meal is what attracts the whole table!

The effect of the Common Denominator is amplified when those people go back to their communities, thanks to the ***Network Effect.*** People with dietary preferences that are typically excluded in the food service industry tend to be highly connected to others who share their dietary preferences. That connection may be in-person, online or both, but it's real and it's powerful.

Parents of children with coeliac disease or severe allergies tend to network online or via in-person support groups. Muslim diners tend to know other Muslim diners. Vegans know other vegans. All of these groups talk amongst themselves about where they go to find food.

Why?

Because *risk* is involved when they choose to eat outside the home.

There's a risk of going hungry if no appropriate food is available. There's a risk of frustration due to poor communication, mis-representation of a menu item, or even just being ignored. And there's the risk of getting sick—or worse—from being served something inappropriate. As a consequence, those with specific dietary preferences are likely to pre-screen places to eat. They may ask others for recommendations in social media groups, or they may choose a business based on the advice of influencers with whom they identify. They will use review websites or apps such as TripAdvisor or, in the case of vegans and allergy sufferers, **HappyCow** and **Teal App,** respectively. And they are very likely to spread the word about their experiences with food service—the good and the bad—in specialized forums.

> **Daniella Levy, Israel—author of *Letters to Josep: An Intro-duction to Judaism***
>
> *"As the mom of a child with coeliac [disease], people don't un-derstand the level of care you have to take with food. You can't have flour floating around in the air.*
>
> *When eating with a group of people, you want to make sure that they know that if you use the knife to spread [something on wheat bread] and you put it back in [the jam, butter, etc.], then he can't eat from that anymore. It's very difficult...for people to understand how strict it needs to be.*
>
> *I follow forums and stuff for coeliacs and parents of coeliacs. They are so appreciative when they come across a place that understands what they need to do and is very careful about it. And we all will flock to that place because we know that we can trust them."*

As a vegan, I definitely benefit from the Network Effect. In turn, I like to help out other vegans. When a business does a great job, I report my experience to vegan social media groups and local face-to-face community groups. I take and share photos of my food, and, if I have a really good time, I deliberately post those pictures further afield on review sites.

It's not just me. People who aren't used to being included get really, really excited when they are. When a business does in-clusivity well, those people will be enthusiastic ambassadors, spreading the word far and wide, because it's a big deal.

Example:
Whilst driving around Iceland for work, I visited a museum in Bor-garnes called The Settlement Center because I was tipped off by someone at Tourist Information that I could possibly eat vegan and have a nice time there. When I arrived, the menu outside didn't tell me much, so I asked a server for details. It turned out the lunch was a vegetarian buffet that was 80% vegan. Even more impres-sively, the server could describe the ingredients in all the dishes and knew precisely which were not suitable for vegans and why.

There was no way I was going to miss out on that! I filled my boots (went back for seconds and small thirds), then had a coffee and dessert. All this, and I wasn't even in need of food because I had eaten breakfast earlier, thinking I wouldn't find anything on the way to my (very far away) destination.

I enjoyed myself so much that I went to the HappyCow app then and there to report this fantastic gem. Six other vegans had been there before me. When the chef came out to chat with me, I showed him the reviews: six five-star reviews, complete with gorgeous pictures of the food. He'd never even heard of Happy-Cow before then. He was thrilled. I have recommended this lovely place every time I hear someone is traveling to Iceland. I hope to go back myself, as I never did get to the museum!

Aimee Louise McKinnon, UK—14 years in executive, head and sous chef positions
"I absolutely love being able to cater for people with dietary requirements. Not only is it nice for them to feel normal, but it's simply excellent for business. Word of mouth is the best advertisement a chef or restaurant can have."

Jackie Norman, New Zealand—author and owner of a PR business and vegan hospitality consultancy
"I think word of mouth is always a wonderful thing. Nobody knows the vegan palate or requirements better than other vegans, and I am a member of lots of Facebook groups based in different regions of the country. I make a note of any highly recommended or often-talked-about eateries in other parts of the country and add them to my 'must-visit' places when I am travelling."

One thing to bear in mind: **The Network Effect also works in the reverse**. If you make someone feel they are an inconvenience because of their dietary preferences, if you get their order wrong, overcharge them, show a lack of knowledge, refuse to serve them, or misrepresent what you can actually offer, they are likely to warn their community not to eat with you. You will be losing them as potential customers, as well as the people they would bring with them and the network to whom they would recommend you.

As with most things in the food service industry, customer service makes all the difference in the world. Dietary minorities are used to being seen as difficult (when they're seen at all!), so **there is a premium amount of goodwill available when you competently include someone who is often excluded.** This fact is the key to understanding how inclusivity efforts can positively impact the perceived exclusivity and prestige of your business.

4.2 How *inclusivity* leads to *exclusivity*

When you do inclusivity well, your customers will spread the word far and wide. The better you do it, the more loudly they sing your praises. By offering—and delivering—what the competition does not, your business becomes more *exclusive*.

Having an inclusive dish on the menu is a good start, especially if it's planned out with the same level of thought given to the rest of the menu. Many customers won't get too excited about a dish of pasta with tomato sauce, for example, even though it might technically tick the boxes for the vegans, the lactose intolerant and many of the allergy sufferers (and even those with coeliacs disease, if you substitute gluten-free pasta). They're also disappointed when their inclusion involves leaving the meat, egg or cheese out of an existing dish but still charging them the full price.

Like all your other customers, those with dietary preferences want to feel that eating out is a treat or an experience. They're hoping for something tasty, satisfying and unique that's also fresh and appealing on the plate. If you want them to rave about you to their communities, go beyond the bare minimum. If you don't, next time they'll go somewhere with more robust and thoughtful options for them.

There's another benefit to planning out an exciting inclusive dish: it's more likely to be something that your typical customer base will also want to sample. An interesting, inclusive menu option is a unique selling point that can boost your prestige with your entire customer base.

4.3 How to initiate the Network Effect and boost your image

1. Do a good job. A really good job. For the Network Effect to happen, people with dietary preferences need to feel considered, included and confident that their experience is not just luck.

> **Nivi Jaswal, US—MBA, NBC-HWC, plant-based investor, non-profit entrepreneur, research innovator, ex-Unilever, Boston Scientific**
> *"I wouldn't walk into a restaurant without first having done my research on the HappyCow app or something else where I'm sure that these people are sensitive, that they're not going to be jerks."*

2. Shout about your capabilities. Make menu adaptations and inclusive dishes obvious and easy to find on menus and signage. Invite customers to enquire about adaptations for dietary preferences. If you don't, people will assume you can't meet their needs. You don't need to cover your menu in allergy information or detailed customization options; Chapter 14 includes subtle cues that those with dietary preferences will recognise as indicators of inclusivity.

3. Be authentically present on review sites and social media. Respond thoughtfully to both positive and negative feedback and be willing to listen and adapt when you have made a mistake. Businesses that ignore complaints or respond badly (aggressively, condescendingly, defensively) suffer for it.

4. Encourage reviews on sites like TripAdvisor, HappyCow and Teal App. HappyCow lets vegans visit any city in the world and have vegan- and vegetarian-friendly options at their fingertips.

The recently released **Teal App** hopes to do for allergy sufferers what HappyCow does for vegans. This all-inclusive app aims to help allergy sufferers live their daily lives safely by pairing emergency features and a food diary with restaurant reviews. You can download their poster for free (**teal.heatherlandex.com**) and post it to encourage allergy sufferers to enjoy the app (and of course review your food outlet, assuming you are allergy-friendly for at least some of the common allergens).

> **James Brooks, UK—founder of Team Brooks, social media marketing for food and beverage brands**
> *"The communities of these minorities are extremely strong and well connected and really prepared to praise brands that are doing a good job. The opportunity is there, if you elevate that with a brand that is engaging with and asking for feedback. Reply to reviews, follow people on social media, see what they are talking about and what they want.*
>
> *The Network Effect can be massive. Of having brand ambassadors who absolutely love you because every time they interact with the brand, you take the time to actually have a personal relationship. You reply to their comments and engage with what they say about your brand. People get a good feeling when they post about you, so they do it more frequently, influencing their social networks. For them, it is relatively rare to be served well."*

Takeaways

- People with dietary preferences network with other Common Denominators.
- The Network Effect amplifies the reach of their reviews and recommendations.
- Go the extra mile. Don't just include people with dietary preferences; treat them with the same level of care and appreciation you have for all your customers.

Free Resources

Links to HappyCow and other free resources are available at
freeresources.heatherlandex.com

Teal App – Download a free colour PDF poster to display in your
outlet at **teal.heatherlandex.com**

More examples, insights and tips are available at
bonuschapter.heatherlandex.com

Part 2

Dietary Preferences:
The Customer Perspective

Part 1 was focused on *why* **inclusivity matters from a business perspective. Part 2 focuses on *what* inclusivity is,** looking at the customer perspective to understand the major dietary preferences that are currently excluded or underserved.

I believe food service is significantly underestimating the number of people with dietary preferences. As stated in Chapter 2, by my estimates, a more accurate global average is anywhere from 20% to 40% of consumers.

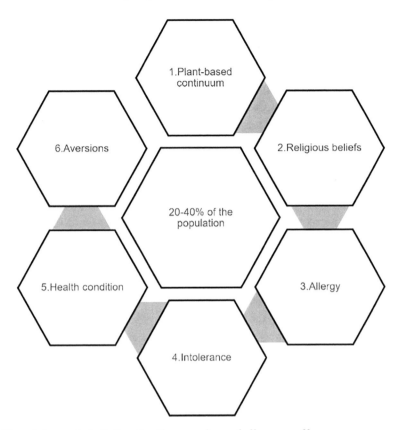

The data and statistics for the number of allergy sufferers, vegans, flexitarians, religious groups and those with food intolerances are not always available, up-to-date or otherwise accurate. However, some trends hold true when comparing data from multiple sources. Specifically, not only is the market bigger than most people in food service estimate it to be, but, **as a whole, that market is growing.**

> **Loui Blake, UK—plant-based investor, restaurant entre-preneur and speaker**
> *"Business owners should be aware just how large the market is for these kinds of foods now. Statistics and studies out there show a growth in gluten-free, vegan, plant-based, pescatarian, etc. Times are hard in food service, and this is an opportunity that shouldn't be ignored. If you don't jump on the bandwagon now, you're going to get left behind."*

Markets in general have changed. Increasing globalisation, freedom of movement and global tourism have increased diversity on a local level over the past years. Populations are now more multinational, multi-ethnic and multi-cultural, which means your local area (i.e., your restaurant catchment area), is changing and will continue to change at a faster and faster pace. Check out the demographic shifts in your catchment area. If you are near a university campus, you may have noticed an even faster pace of change. Younger generations are driving more of the change than previous generations, due to a combination of factors including technology and social media use, environmental and personal health concerns, and the rise in diagnosed allergies and intolerances.

These trends may surprise you. When surveying your customers, you see the world through tinted glasses. **You cannot see the people you are not serving.** If you have not taken steps toward inclusivity, you rarely glimpse the market of those with dietary preferences. Those individuals have either found other places to go or made the choice to stay home.

An important note on motivations for dietary preferences

We have already established that allergies are one possible reason for a customer's dietary preferences. However, if you take away only one idea from Part 2 of this book, I hope it is that **other dietary preferences should be taken just as seriously as allergies.**

As you'll see here in Part 2 when I discuss different intolerances and sensitivities, non-allergic adverse reactions to foods (e.g., coeliac disease, lactose intolerance) can be quite consequential and include symptoms similar to food poisoning. In some cases, those symptoms can last for days or weeks. These reactions can be very costly for the customer in terms of physical suffering and inconvenience. In some cases, they will necessitate time off work. However, few businesses treat other dietary preferences with the care they give to those with allergies. As a result, some customers feel pushed to do whatever they can to convince the business to take their preference seriously.

Anonymous
I have to lie in restaurants and say I am allergic to butter. They can manage dairy-free, but then they roll it in butter before they serve it to me. I feel very naughty saying I'm allergic, but I have to because when I don't, I get ill.

The quote above—taken from one of the interviews I conducted for this book—is an example of what I call an "***allegedy***" (alleged allergy). This person doesn't have a diagnosed allergy, but they claim they do to ensure they get food which won't make them sick. Terminology for intolerances and sensitivities can be confusing, and the customer has no guarantee that a given business will understand their specific medical concern or condition. The word "allergy" is generally better understood, and it triggers a set of procedures and protocols in the kitchen that can result in better outcomes for the customer.

From a customer service perspective, you don't need to know whether the customer has an allergy or an allegedy. There is nothing to gain by assuming the customer has an allegedy, and there's a lot at risk if you are wrong.

If a customer says they have an allergy, your responsibility is to provide food that meets the needs they've specified and ensure there's no ***contamination*** (i.e., stuff or traces of stuff in the food that the customer doesn't want in the food)[2] in the kitchen. If you can't do that, be honest.

That's how you create a great customer experience. And a great customer experience is the first, essential step to leveraging the Common Denominator and Network Effects.

---

2   *Allergen contamination is officially called "cross-contact" in food service to distinguish it from "cross-contamination", which often makes food handlers think of bacteria controls. In this book, I use the term contamination, as it is often not microscopic amounts but rather accidental amounts.*

Inclusivity is exceptional customer service. **Period.**

Inclusivity isn't really new, complicated or different. It's a specific version of what smart businesses have been doing all along.

Consider the facts:

🔖 **Inclusivity means knowing your product and how it's prepared.** A server at a Michelin-starred restaurant is expected to be able to explain the dishes on the menu, right down to the sourcing of the ingredients. In the same way, a business aiming for inclusivity will train its staff to be able to guide customers to the options appropriate for their dietary preferences. Servers will know the processes in the back of the house well enough to explain them to customers for whom contamination is a concern.

🔖 **Inclusivity means understanding your customer's profile.** You don't need to be an expert in any single dietary preference, but being aware of the major differences between them goes a long way. Is the customer who asks whether the biscuits on the breakfast buffet are dairy-free asking because they don't eat animal products, because they are allergic to cow's milk protein or because they are lactose intolerant? Knowing that—and knowing your product!—will enable you to tell them what they need to know about the biscuits and also guide them to other appropriate options on the buffet (including spreads, dips, toppings and dressings).

🔖 **Inclusivity means listening to the customer, communicating your capabilities clearly and doing your best to accommodate their preferences.** The motivations behind dietary preferences are complex, and individuals will vary in how flexible they are with their diets. As mentioned above, **your responsibility is to ensure the customer can make an informed decision. The decision is theirs.**

❧ **Inclusivity means considering who you might be missing or excluding and doing your best to create a menu with robust options for them.** Go beyond the minimum. Offer a full dining experience with tasty, thoughtfully developed drinks, starters, entrees and desserts.

❧ **Inclusivity means making information available without making the customer feel like a burden.** Signage in a bakery or deli indicating whether options are vegan or kosher, for example. Easy-to-read inclusivity cues on printed menus. Filter functions for online menus. Notices on the website and social media pages directing customers with dietary preferences to further information or encouraging them to call ahead to ask about options. A friendly note on the menu inviting customers to ask how dishes could be modified to meet specific dietary preferences.

And on and on and on. All of the examples given above are indicators of ***outstanding customer service.*** They give customers confidence in food safety standards. There is no better way to drive organic, word-of-mouth marketing for these normally excluded minority groups.

From here, we're going to explore the specifics of a variety of dietary preferences. I want to equip you with the knowledge you need to start thinking about what would be required to effectively include more of these different groups in your business. **Remember: the goal is to be as inclusive as possible, given your specific resources and circumstances, to increase your capacity and capabilities in the long term.**

Chapter 4

The Curse of Knowledge

In this chapter:
The Curse of Knowledge
Systems for safety
The Dunning-Kruger Effect

5.1 The Curse of Knowledge

"We cannot imagine what it would be like not to possess the knowledge we now have, and this means that we cannot put ourselves in the place of the listener."
–Morten Munsten in his 2019 book I'm Afraid Debbie from Marketing Has Left for the Day

The Curse of Knowledge **is a knowledgeable person's tendency to overestimate how much of what they say is understood when discussing their area of knowledge with another person.** Experts may be too technical, jargon-heavy or academic when explaining, or their experience and knowledge may make it hard for them to consider what a non-expert needs to know to follow along. Put simply: when they talk, they aren't being understood by the listener, and they may have no idea. It's a natural human flaw, and it happens often among food safety compliance professionals, food businesses and people with dietary preferences because *each of them can be experts in their own domain.*

The Curse of Knowledge works from me to you, from you to your staff, and between your staff and your customers. Servers may struggle with specific terms, like what is or is not halal or vegan. Your customers may not know how a commercial kitchen works or the best procedure for ordering a modified dish from your menu. Your staff may also use different terminology for dietary preferences, depending on where and when they learnt about them. Staff may assume the customer understands when they don't, and vice versa.

Example:
While staying in a hotel in Denmark with a good breakfast buffet, I asked the woman attending the buffet whether the bread was vegan. She appeared unsure of the term, so I gave her the simplified explanation that I meant without egg or milk. She investigated and came back quite satisfied that all the bread on the buffet was lactose-free. I said, "Is it made with lactose-free milk or without milk? And what about egg?"

She went to investigate again. This time when she came back, she told me I could only have pre-packaged gluten-free breakfast biscuits. Fortunately, the buffet also offered oat milk and muesli without milk powder added. (I like it when buffets offer the oats, granola, seeds, nuts and dried fruit all separately, which they often do at this hotel chain—or did, pre-pandemic. This kind of separation makes it much easier for people with dietary preferences to make their own combinations.)

I was a bit disappointed about the bread, but it was my mistake. I had overestimated how much she knew about allergens based on the availability of gluten- and lactose-free items on the buffet, including plant-based milk and yoghurt. But the attendant is far from alone. Much confusion occurs with the terms *milk-free, non-dairy, dairy-free* and *lactose-free*. (More on that in Chapter 6.)

> **Tarryn Gorre, UK—CEO and co-founder of Kafoodle, a food-tech company matching people to food within the education, hospitality and healthcare spaces**
> *Another problem we have is that consumers communicate things in different ways. Whether it's an allergy, dislike or intolerance; gluten-free, coeliac or barley issue; legumes; dairy; whether we are talking about eggs or milk.*

To help with this issue, I discuss dietary preference terms in depth here in Part 2, and I have provided a glossary at the back of the book. However, you don't need every person in your company hierarchy to become experts in nutrition, immunology, medicine, food technology, or even how the food is prepared, manufactured, stored, tested, labelled, etc.

To provide excellent customer service, risk less and earn more, ***each person does need a system in which they know their role and understand the "why" behind it.***

5.2 About that system...

By necessity, food safety in a commercial kitchen is extremely different to food safety in the home, where the risk of injuring many people is limited. In commercial kitchens, systems matter.

Individual staff members can assume less overall responsibility as long as someone—such as the manager, head chef, supervisor, or owner (if they are present on site)—takes it. The system(s) has to be a well-oiled machine, and all staff have to be onboard with following procedures carefully. Finally, the system must be kept up to date and monitored for compliance.

Why?

Safety is only as good as the system on which it depends, but the system alone is not enough. As a consultant, I can only advise and/or create the system and tools and/or train staff. I cannot ensure the system is running correctly and updated daily. Likewise, the software programs used to manage ingredients, allergies, bookings or orders are only supports. The user of these tools is still responsible for using them correctly, and the business operator is still responsible for compliance and mistakes.

Here's an example of how a system that's incomplete or not kept up to date can fail:

> **Mark Morgan-Huntley, UK—chef, founder and director of Allergen Checker Ltd. allergenchecker.co.uk**
> *Allergen Checker [software that helps chefs manage allergens through printed labels and menus] started as an idea when the new allergen labelling law came into effect in the UK in 2014. As a chef, I looked at it from the other side—how can chefs complete all this required documentation? Chefs don't want to be snowed under by excessive amounts of paperwork.*
>
> *All that was brought out by the Food Standards Agency was a form with a simple tick box to show what allergens are in each dish on the menu. **Daily specials tend to be forgotten about,** as the form has already been completed for the menu.*

A dish served without allergen accounting and disclosure is a risk, and efforts toward inclusivity should always be focused on reducing risk—for both the customer and the business.

5.3 Training and the Dunning-Kruger Effect

Robust training is an essential part of becoming more inclusive. The **way** you train employees about dietary preferences also matters, as you want to avoid staff falling victim to the **Dunning-Kruger Effect.**

The Dunning-Kruger Effect (Kruger & Dunning, 1999), named for the two psychologists who came up with the concept, describes a cognitive bias phenomenon where people with relatively low ability at a task overestimate their proficiency. In other words, they will soon learn what they don't yet know.

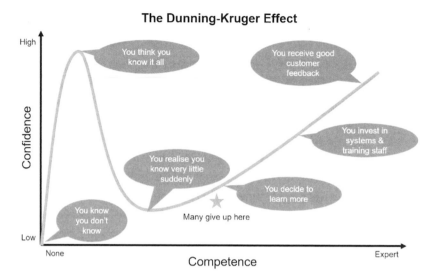

The Dunning-Kruger Effect

I've made the diagram above to illustrate how the Dunning-Kruger Effect can look in food service. Consider food allergies. Say a staff member starts off knowing nothing about food allergies. They then learn a bit on the subject through allergy awareness training and come to feel they have a good grasp on the subject. In reality, however, they cannot yet reliably identify potential risks to those with allergies, or they underestimate how complicated and variable allergies can be from one individual to the next.

Unfortunately, the first time this staff member realizes how much they still have to learn may be when something goes wrong. Not only does this put the customer (and the business) at risk, but it may leave you stuck at the star in the diagram above, lacking the motivation to be more inclusive now that allergy management suddenly appears overwhelmingly complicated or difficult.

My advice to every business with whom I consult: If you are at the stage where you know you don't know, go ahead and skip over the stage where you think you know it all. Come join me in the "Decide to learn more" stage.

I have learnt a great deal about food allergies, intolerances, religiously motivated diets and dietary preferences generally, but this learning is life-long. I will continue seeking out new information in order to stay up to date as knowledge and best practices change.

Why it's worth committing to regular, ongoing training and development

- Staff are better able to remember the details of their training.
- Training will reflect up-to-date information.
- Staff are less likely to mistake the good overview they get in a high-quality training with genuine expertise.
- Your progress toward inclusivity will be less affected by staff turnover or other staffing challenges such as temporary/seasonal staff, agency staff, event staff or part-time employees.

No one person can know everything. Not even experts. But we can learn quite a lot if we make continuous improvement the goal.

Takeaways

- Consider where you are on the Dunning-Kruger Curve when speaking or listening to others.
- All staff must know why they should be more inclusive and their role in a well-functioning system.

Free Resources

See Author Recommended Resources at the back of the book for more info from **Allergen Checker Ltd.**
You can find links to articles, statistics, campaigns and other free resources at **freeresources.heatherlandex.com**

Chapter 6

Lactose Intolerance

In this chapter:
What is lactose intolerance?
What food service can do

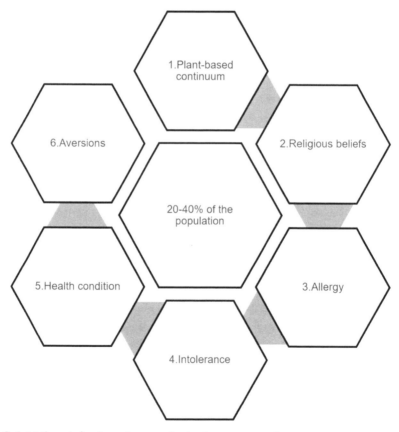

1.Plant-based continuum

6.Aversions

2.Religious beliefs

20-40% of the population

5.Health condition

3.Allergy

4.Intolerance

6.1 What is lactose intolerance?

Lactose intolerance (LI) is the inability of the body to digest lactose, which is a naturally occurring sugar in milk and dairy products. Typical symptoms can include gastrointestinal discomfort, diarrhoea, nausea (and sometimes vomiting), abdominal cramps, bloating and gas.

**Lactose intolerance can be debilitating.
Symptoms of LI:**

Not everyone with lactose intolerance has been diagnosed as such, or they may be misdiagnosed with another condition, such as irritable bowel syndrome (IBS). Whether diagnosed or not, many of those with lactose intolerance will be aware of a sensitivity to milk and milk products, but LI is not the same as milk/dairy intolerance or milk allergy, both of which are a reaction to a protein in milk, not lactose.

Lactose intolerance is far from atypical. After babies are weaned from their mothers' milk, it is genetically normal for them to become increasingly lactose intolerant as they grow, because their ability to produce lactase (which breaks down lactose) declines.

"About 70% of the world's population suffer from LI due to a genetically programmed gradual decline in lactase expression after weaning, so-called lactase non-persistence."
–Heine et al., 2017, in the *World Allergy Organisation Journal*

As Heine et al. state, around seventy per cent of the world population is estimated to be lactose intolerant. However, rates of lactose intolerance vary among different populations. It is most common in those of African descent, Hispanics/Latinos and Asians (up to 100%), while it is least common in people of European descent (approximately 10%).

Many people who are symptomatic find they can manage lactose intolerance fairly easily by taking an enzyme pill or probiotic supplement that helps them break down the lactose in traditional (i.e., lactose-containing) dairy products.

Of course, timing the pill correctly depends on the customer *knowing* they are eating a lactose-containing product!

If people with severe lactose intolerance unknowingly consume food containing milk, either due to an undisclosed ingredient or contamination in the kitchen, they may experience symptoms similar to food poisoning.

Remember, "contamination" in this context just means that something is in the food that the customer doesn't want there. What we may consider an ordinary or non-problematic ingredient can be very problematic for some customers.

Example:
I recently bought a vegan toasted sandwich in a coffee chain of which I am particularly fond. Halfway through eating the sandwich, I discovered that it had someone else's melted cheese on the base of it. Yes, there were "consequences" for me, despite taking my vegan lactase pills when I arrived home. My body is no longer used to digesting animal fats or lactose.

My experience is not unique. Because diet affects a person's gut bacteria, many vegans become or return to being naturally lactose intolerant over time as their digestive systems go back to genetically programmed low levels of lactase. As a result, an otherwise fantastic vegan meal contaminated with milk, cheese or any dairy product can have undesired side effects. Although I started to feel better within a few hours after taking my lactase pills, other intolerances are more severe and may cause greater injury or symptoms that last days or weeks.

6.2 What does this mean in the context of food service?
The simple version:
- Know what products you offer contain milk
- Maintain organized records of allergens and ingredients
- Ensure you have and effectively communicate milk-free options, including possible modifications, in all sections on the menu

♦ Establish and maintain procedures in the kitchen that ensure food is not contaminated with unwanted ingredients

Why milk-free? Would it be enough to offer dishes made with lactose-free milk or cheese?

In lactose-free dairy products, lactase is added directly to traditional cow's milk to neutralize the lactose before additional processing or consumption. And, yes, that would be suitable for the lactose-intolerant individuals. But it would not work for your vegans, who want to avoid all products of animal origin. It would also not work for anyone with a milk allergy. To streamline safe processes and maximize profits, I recommend finding options that can serve as many dietary preferences as possible. (More on that later!)

Tip: The terms *non-dairy* and *dairy-free* are not interchangeable. *Dairy-free* is guaranteed milk-free and thus suitable for vegans and those with milk allergy. *Non-dairy* products, however, may contain milk proteins or derivatives. For inclusive options, always choose milk-free.

Takeaways
♦ The way your customers understand and talk about their intolerances may vary.
♦ LI is extremely common across the world.
♦ The symptoms of LI can be painful and significant.

Free Resources
You can find links to articles, statistics, campaigns and other free resources at **freeresources.heatherlandex.com**

Chapter 7

Gluten Intolerance & Coeliac Disease

In this chapter:

What is gluten?
Coeliac disease and gluten intolerance
What food service can do
The challenges of packaged goods

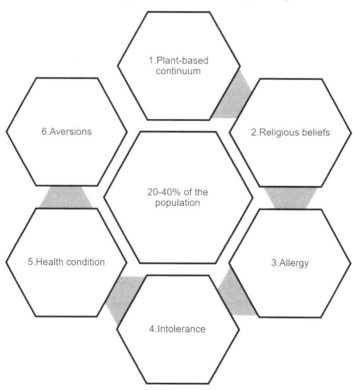

Make no mistake: the gluten-free market is huge.
"The global gluten-free products market size was estimated at USD 21.61 billion in 2019 and is expected to expand at a CAGR of 9.2% during the forecast period of 2020 to 2027."
—Grand View Research, 2020

7.1 What is gluten?

Gluten is a protein found in certain cereals, including wheat.
Anyone who has ever kneaded traditional wheat dough has done so to develop the sticky, stretchy gluten proteins that give bread its structure.

7.2 What is coeliac disease?

Coeliac disease (or "celiac disease" in the US) is an autoimmune disease triggered by gluten. When a person with coeliac disease ingests gluten, the body's immune system mistakenly begins to attack healthy tissue, leading to damage on the lining of the intestine. Symptoms can vary from one individual to the next and range from diarrhoea and stomach aches to rashes, malnutrition, nerve damage and more. According to Coeliac UK, the disease is life-long, can only be managed by avoiding gluten and occurs in about one out of every hundred people.

Is coeliac disease different from gluten intolerance?
Yes. Gluten intolerance, also called non-coeliac gluten sensitivity, may have similar symptoms, but there is little to no intestinal damage, and new research suggests that the cause may be bigger than gluten alone.

*FODMAPs, a group of poorly digested carbohydrates, may be the cause of the symptoms [of gluten sensitivity] instead. **It is also important to note that wheat, barley and rye—gluten-containing grains—are all high in FODMAPs.***
—Beyond Celiac, 2021

According to the Beyond Celiac patient advocacy organization, around 18 million Americans have gluten sensitivity/intolerance, which is six times the number with coeliac disease. **Six per cent of the American population** have a legitimate problem with gluten. Despite its reputation in some circles, gluten intolerance is neither a fantasy nor a fad.

Where does wheat allergy fit in?
Wheat allergy is an immune reaction to any of the many other proteins in wheat. An allergic reaction to wheat may involve skin rashes, swelling or itching in or around the mouth, lung irritation or difficulty breathing (including potentially fatal anaphylaxis), or gastrointestinal problems. Those with wheat protein allergy have to avoid wheat, but they may tolerate other cereals containing gluten (such as barley or rye) perfectly well.

So is gluten an allergen or not?
Medically, no. Without going into the details of immunology, the autoimmune response gluten triggers in someone with coeliac disease is different to the immune response to an allergen. However, to simplify legislation for labelling requirements in the EU, **the allergens listed in the EU 14 include *"cereals containing gluten",*** such as barley, rye or wheat. (More on allergies in Chapter 8.)

7.3 What does this mean in the context of food service?

You have three different conditions to think about when offering gluten-free. Depending on what conditions are driving someone's request for a gluten-free meal, one person may accept "traces" of gluten, while others would be very ill or suffer anaphylaxis (if the gluten-containing cereal were wheat). **Talk to your customers.** You don't need to know all the details driving customers' dietary preferences. You do need to understand how to serve them safely.

As a baseline, my advice is to treat gluten intolerance and coeliac disease the same (that is, strictly gluten-free), and address allergies according to the customer's specific requests (e.g., wheat-, barley-, spelt- or rye-free).

Note

Some naturally gluten-free grains may contain gluten from cross-contact with gluten-containing grains during harvesting and/or processing. Oats are a common example, which is why some customers may ask whether your granola or oatmeal is gluten-free. Although oats do not naturally contain gluten, there is a high risk of contamination unless you ensure you are purchasing oats labelled and sold as gluten-free, a claim requiring that gluten does not exceed 20 parts per million.

Only guarantee customers that food is gluten- or allergen-free if you can guarantee it *absolutely.* While this may mean you cannot serve them, that is often not the case. There are significantly more individuals with gluten intolerance than with coeliac disease, for example. There are also people who are trying to cut down on gluten for other reasons. So the customer may come back to you and say that they can tolerate small amounts of gluten, or that they will accept "may contain" on a label if the risk is low. Remember: **Your responsibility is to ensure the customer can make an informed decision. The decision is theirs.**

Example:

CEO of an international pizza chain (anonymous)

We do a gluten-free option.

As a business it is really quite challenging catering to the needs of allergy sufferers and people with particular diets because there's no room for error. In a high-volume business, where things move quite fast, it can be difficult. There's a moral responsibility because it can be life-threatening to some people, or at least make them quite sick. That's a lot to deal with. We have to have really strong rules.

Gluten-free is probably 1% of our product base. So, it's tiny in the overall picture, and it's a lot of work. Our gluten-free procedures are tough.

We only sell two types of gluten-free pizza, a margherita and a pepperoni. One of our rules is that staff cannot use anything that is already in the makeline [because we want to avoid contamination with wheat flour]. Another rule is because of that, you cannot modify the pizza, and that makes people really angry.

They get very, very upset.

Many of our customers say, "Yeah, I just don't want gluten, but I don't care if there is a little bit in there." However, if we are busy, it is impossible for us to determine that order by order. The system is built for an allergy sufferer or someone with a dietary requirement, so the personalization conversation is really hard to have in the middle of a rush.

To a business in this situation, I would suggest a small statement on the menu: *When ordering a gluten-free pizza, only our pepperoni and margherita are gluten-free. All other toppings likely contain gluten. Please ask for more information.* The staff could then repeat this statement when the customer starts a gluten-free order for any pizza other than the pepperoni or margherita. The goal is for staff to quickly and confidently differentiate between customers that are ordering a gluten-free pizza and those that are ordering a standard pizza with a gluten-free base. The first group need a contamination-free meal. The second group, which I would call "gluten reducers", just want to cut down on the amount of gluten they are consuming.

It is possible to find a way for the gluten reducers to have their pizza without increasing a business' liability. Obviously, there are operational considerations, training requirements, and costing for the gluten-free base, but I am sad to see efforts aimed at properly including the 1% of the population with coeliac disease potentially cost a business the 6% of the population who *might* accept "may contain" or "traces of", not to mention all the others who just want to reduce gluten consumption for other reasons.

Remember, inclusion is about excellent customer service.

Jacqui McPeake, UK—owner of JACS Ltd. (food allergen and catering specialists) and former head of catering at a large university

There was one dinner where everyone would get up and change seats to network. Eight of them had different dietary requests, so we had to follow these people around the room. One was gluten intolerant, strict instructions not to give her any gluten. On this particular occasion, it was lamb chops with a breaded coating, so her chop was a plain one. I couldn't find her at first. When I finally did, she was sitting at another table eating the breaded lamb. She said, "It's ok. I am fine with a bit." I went back to the kitchen and the chefs were complaining: "We've been catering for her for years, and she's ok!"

I said, "Actually, a person with a gluten intolerance knows their intolerance." She probably hadn't had any for a few days and thought she might get mild discomfort but was ok to eat it. Other people, those with a severe intolerance, could be really poorly after any slight bread crumb.

*I said to my team, **"It's not up to us to decide how far along the scale she is from one to ten. We haven't got time to stand here discussing it—we're too busy. Just assume the worst-case scenario every time."***

7.4 A quick word about packaged foods from the experts

José Luis Cabañero, Spain—founder and CEO at Eatable Adventures, a global food innovation hub

There is not a solid public education on gluten-free labelling. I recently had an interaction with a journalist who was annoyed because of the abundance of gluten-free labelling in CPGs (Consumer Packaged Goods). She thought this was a commercial tactic to increase sales. My take was focused on how difficult it is for someone with coeliac disease to have to read and understand all the ingredients in a specific food label. On many occasions, wheat is buried in the ingredient list, and it's not clear which allergen ingredients your food contains.

I think that it is helpful to have labels at least on the back of packaging or in an allergy matrix which make clear statements for the general public such as "Suitable for coeliacs" or "Naturally gluten-free", much like the "Suitable for vegans and vegetarians" label. Such labels seem less likely to scare off more typical eaters (who may be concerned the food will not taste as good), and they make life easier for those buying or preparing food, especially if those people are not practiced at ordering or shopping for individuals with gluten-free diets.

People who find themselves suddenly on a gluten-free diet either temporarily (as part of an elimination diet for diagnosis) or as a result of a new diagnosis don't necessarily know how to prepare gluten-free meals or read labels. These aren't universally taught skills. They must be learnt. Similarly, customers eating out need to understand what is in their food. If they are new to a gluten-free diet, they may not yet have thought about all the places where gluten may "hide", such as in soy sauce, muesli, special seasonings or soups. ***Make it easy for people to see what options are available.***

Takeaways

🖊 It is helpful to state something is "naturally gluten-free" when it is.

🖊 Be honest if you cannot guarantee a dish is absolutely gluten- or wheat-free. There is a gradient, and there is also a gradient in what a customer will accept.

🖊 Gluten may be hidden in ingredients. Understand that allergy labelling can be a bit more difficult for gluten.

Free Resources

You can find links to articles, statistics, campaigns and other free resources at **freeresources.heatherlandex.com**

Chapter 8

Food Allergies

In this chapter:
The allergy crisis
What is an allergy?
Intolerances and aversions
Labelling requirements
What food service can do
Creating a win-win

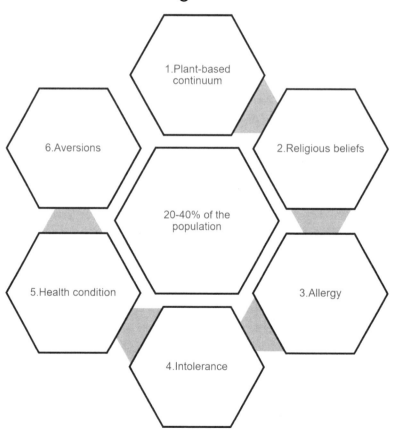

1.Plant-based continuum

6.Aversions

2.Religious beliefs

20-40% of the population

5.Health condition

3.Allergy

4.Intolerance

8.1 How widespread are allergies?

It's a modern phenomenon. There is an "Allergy Crisis".
It doesn't matter whether you look at the National Health Service in the UK, the Center for Disease Control in the US, the World Health Organization, the World Allergy Organization or the Australasian Society of Clinical Immunology and Allergy: all are reporting more people with food allergies and more cases of anaphylaxis. The common estimates of those living with food allergies (extrapolated from the sources above) are 2 million in the UK, 32 million in the United States, 7 million in Europe and 1 billion worldwide. And the number of people with allergies is increasing rapidly. Although the cause is unknown, hypotheses include pollution levels, chemicals and additives in our food, exposure to "exotic" or novel foods our direct ancestors would not have encountered, over-sanitisation (the "Hygiene Hypothesis"), nutritional deficiencies, stress, lifestyle issues and/or some combination of the above. As the food chain has grown increasingly complex, so, too, have allergies.

"It is generally accepted that food allergy affects approximately 2.5% of the general population, but the spread of prevalence data is wide, ranging from 1% to 10%."
—**World Allergy Organisation, 2017**

"It is estimated that between 1–10% of adults and children have a food hypersensitivity. However **as many as 20% of the population experience some reactions to foods** *which make them believe they do have a food hypersensitivity."*
—**British Dietetic Association, 2021**

If you are the owner of a restaurant, this means that up to 10% of your customers may have a food allergy.

One out of ten!
As I've mentioned earlier in this book, statistics will vary based on your local population. However, the key takeaway is that there

may be a great many more people in your area living with food allergies than you first thought. That's even without factoring in those who have an intolerance or some other unfavourable consequence from eating a certain food, which the above quote from Allergy UK estimates at up to **20% of the population**.

How many people in your catchment population could be pleased, feel more confident, give great feedback and become loyal repeat customers if you increased and promoted the allergy-friendliness of your restaurant?

8.2 What is an allergy?

According to the American Academy of Allergy, Asthma and Immunology, an allergy is "a chronic condition involving an abnormal reaction to an ordinarily harmless substance called an allergen". When we talk about food allergies, it's usually proteins causing this atypical immune response.

Other terms may be used in connection with allergies, such as:
- food hypersensitivity (food allergy),
- food sensitivity (intolerance),
- immune-mediated intolerance (an autoimmune problem in the gut) and anaphylaxis (severe, potentially fatal allergic reaction).

You don't really need to know what specialists call all the many types of allergies or allergic reactions. You do need to know that if a customer (or staff member) tells you they have an allergy, *listen to them, take it seriously and learn more.* To help, I have put together the glossary and bibliography at the back of this book, as well as many other resources at *freeresources.heatherlandex.com.*

Not all allergies or intolerances have equal consequences. It's a gradient of severity of potential injury with many contributing factors. Intolerances and coeliac disease can be very severe, and some food allergies can be mild.

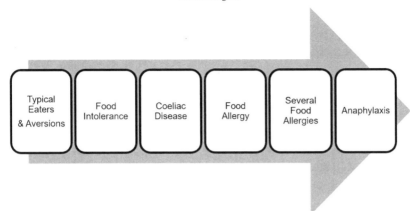

Allergies can also be triggered differently from one individual to the next. Some people must ingest (eat or drink) the allergen before they will experience a reaction, but others may react to certain allergens via skin contact or inhalation of small airborne particles.

Allergy symptoms can include hives, itching, eczema, swelling (lips, mouth, tongue), breathing difficulties, asthma, rhinitis (inflammation in the nose), abdominal pain, diarrhoea, vomiting or anaphylaxis (with the possibility of severe injury or death).

Reactions can be immediate or delayed several days. People may manage allergic reactions with steroids, immunosuppressants, antihistamines, nasal sprays, eye drops or, in the case of anaphylaxis, an automatic epinephrine injector (commonly known by the brand name EpiPen).

In food service, safely serving individuals with allergies means **knowing what's in the food** (including all ingredients and ingredient components), **clearly disclosing what's in it** and **ensuring no contamination happens during preparation or service**.

If you don't feel confident in your own knowledge of allergy management, learning more is worth the required investment of time, energy and money.

8.3 A quick note on intolerances and aversions

Intolerances, also called "food sensitivities", are perhaps even more difficult to pinpoint and diagnose than allergies...and that's saying something. In some cases, they *are* undiagnosed allergies. In 2020, **Uptodate, a clinical decision resource,** reported that 15–20% of the UK population have a food intolerance (not including diagnosed allergies), but figures vary quite a bit. Very little data on intolerances is available, perhaps because intolerances, while uncomfortable and sometimes debilitating, are generally not believed to trigger life-threatening anaphylaxis. As a result, people with intolerances, after hopefully ruling out allergies with their doctor, may simply change their eating habits and give up on seeking a diagnosis altogether.

The full picture of adverse, atypical reactions to food is beyond the scope of this book. The important takeaway is that **intolerances are managed the same way as allergies: by avoiding the foods or additives that trigger the reaction.**

A *food aversion,* in contrast, is a powerful dislike of a specific food based on how that individual perceives the sight, smell, texture or taste. Some people may be repulsed by even the idea of a certain food. Food aversions may so strong that they make people ill (e.g., vomit), but their symptoms are psychologically driven, not allergic reactions or physical intolerances.

Food aversions can occur in response to any food and at any point in one's life. They may be temporary (as in during pregnancy) or ongoing.

Some food aversions are tied to culturally specific ideas around what is "normal" and "abnormal" to eat and may include specific animals or parts of the animal, insects, fermented or cultured foods, foods eaten raw versus cooked, fungi and more.

What do those in food service need to know?

Jacqui McPeake, UK—owner of JACS Ltd. (food allergen and catering specialist), former head of catering at a large university
People are allowed to not like things. That is hard for some chefs to appreciate.

That's it. Really.

You don't need to know why they won't eat something, and you don't need to try to figure out whether or not you think they actually might be able to eat some amount of it.

Listen to your customers. Be honest about your capabilities and limitations, and serve people to the best of your abilities.

Listened-to customers are loyal customers.

8.4 Legal obligations for labelling

Allergen[3] disclosure rules vary around the world. The EU has relatively extensive requirements, with food labelling legislation covering *fourteen allergens*: milk, egg, soya, sesame, cereals containing gluten, lupin, sulphur dioxide/sulphites, fish, crustaceans, molluscs, nuts, peanuts, mustard, celery.

Canada has eleven: eggs, milk, mustard, peanuts, crustaceans and molluscs, fish, sesame seeds, soy, sulphites, tree nuts, wheat (including triticale, a hybrid of wheat).

In the **US, there are the "Big Eight"**: milk, eggs, fish, crustacean shellfish, tree nuts, peanuts, wheat and soybeans.

Of course, people can be allergic to absolutely anything, which is part of what can make allergy diagnosis so challenging. The allergens above are relatively common, which is why they are included in legislation. However, individual businesses may go above and beyond the legal minimum to list and manage other allergens or ingredients of concern. In a world-famous workplace cafeteria in the EU, I have witnessed clear labelling of nineteen different ingredients (including pork, beef and alcohol). Such labelling is aimed at being more inclusive for their international work force, which I assume is a good strategy for retaining staff.

Labelling is valuable and necessary for individuals with allergies, but it's also more broadly helpful for inclusivity. It's also likely to expand. For example, in November 2020, the US

---

3   *Reminder: An allergen is the thing in food (usually a protein) that causes an allergic reaction in a sensitive individual (the allergy sufferer).*

Food and Drug Administration released draft guidance for the voluntary disclosure of sesame as an allergen in the US.

8.5 What does this mean in the context of food service?

Inclusivity is challenging when it comes to individuals with allergies. To start with, even the relatively short lists of foods covered under allergy legislation can be difficult to understand, and customers and food service staff alike may be at odds trying to understand whether a specific ingredient poses an allergen risk to a customer. For example, "shellfish" includes molluscs like squid, octopuses and cuttlefish, which are often forgotten since they don't have an obvious shell. But molluscs also include both land and water snails, which otherwise seem to have nothing to do with the sea creatures in the "shellfish" category.

Nuts are another common source of confusion and conflict. Peanuts, despite the name, are not nuts at all, but legumes like peas and lentils. It's not uncommon to be allergic to both tree nuts and peanuts, however, and people may avoid both even if they're only allergic to one. (Nuts are often processed in the same facility, increasing the risk of contamination.) And what about coconuts? Technically drupes (nut, seed and fruit in one), coconuts are not one of the EU allergens, but the US Food and Drug Administration classifies it as a tree nut. Individuals with nut allergies may react to coconuts, but not necessarily.

Adding to the complication of safe allergy management is that it **requires attention to procedures and risks beyond the walls of your business.** Contamination can occur during harvesting and processing before the food reaches you (think "may contain" and "traces of" warnings on packaging). If you are looking to prepare a meal for someone with severe allergies, you must also investigate and communicate these risks.

> **Note**
> Although the consumer is the best source of information about their specific needs, they may not understand food labelling, disclaimers of risk, or the risk of food being contaminated with allergens in processing facilities or commercial kitchens.

Julian Edwards, UK—CEO at Allergen Accreditation
The biggest challenge is cross-contamination in the kitchen. To keep workstations sanitised and cleaned is essential whenever different ingredients are being prepped. That applies to equipment as well; for example, using a griddle to do a fish item and then immediately using it for meat. It's fine from a general food safety sense, but you are depositing allergens which will contaminate other foods unless the equipment is cleaned between uses.

Mark Morgan-Huntley, UK—chef, founder & director of Allergen Checker Ltd., software to help chefs manage allergens through printed labels and menus allergen-checker.co.uk
*Education is the key here. It's about teaching people to understand that they **have to do it**. It is the law and whatever the chef puts on a plate could potentially cause a serious reaction or, even worse, a fatality. It's about getting in the mindset of "**I must have an easy-to-use system to safeguard my business and my customers.**"*

The difficulty of effectively training an entire staff on the issues above is a legitimate practical concern, though well-designed systems (and regular, rigorous compliance checks!) can go a long way. Even so, food service businesses must overcome significant challenges to serve allergy sufferers. My goal is to show you how many customers you may be missing out on and help you evaluate whether your business is currently in a position to invest in the effort and education required to protect against adverse incidents, so you can safely reach this largely untapped market.

8.6 Is it possible to create a win-win for customers and your business?

It is definitely possible to improve allergy practices to protect both your business and your customers. Just like with all other aspects of inclusivity, you must 1) understand exactly what your customer is seeking, 2) know what's in your food and communicate that clearly, 3) only promise what you can deliver *absolutely* and 4) ensure safe preparation practices (allergen control) that guard against contamination.

An example of the risk of overpromising:

My friend Alice has a severe peanut allergy, which includes the risk of anaphylaxis. Last year, I took her to a specific café because I'd chatted with the owner during a previous visit and she'd said they were "peanut-free". I thought it would be perfect for both of us. The vegan options were amazing, and the owner had food allergies herself, so I was confident in her evaluation of what "peanut-free" meant. But when we arrived, Alice noticed that peanut butter was listed as an ingredient in one of their smoothies *and* in one of the brunch offerings.

Alice told me that she was a little worried when she read it, but quickly clarified, "It's always like that, though."

Whilst we were there, I spoke to the lady who makes their glorious vegan raw cakes. "You're nut-free, right?"

Her reply: "Oh yeah. *Most of the time, I don't use nuts.*"

Nuts and peanuts are not the same, as we've discussed, but nuts often pose risk to those with peanut allergies because they may be processed in the same factories. And, at least in Alice's case, there was additional risk hiding in a place I never would have expected: hummus. Hummus is typically made with chickpeas, lemon juice, garlic, olive oil...and a sesame seed paste known as tahini.

Alice's years of managing her allergy in restaurants meant that she was an expert in her own condition, so she knew to ask whether the hummus contained tahini. It did. Alice later told me that there were things she had learnt to avoid because they were often contaminated with traces of peanut. Tahini, she explained, is almost always made in factories which also produce peanut butter.

My friend Alice was fine (fortunately!) because she had a lot of experience managing her allergy, and she had learnt enough about food processing and preparation to spot potential red flags. **But overpromising—or not understanding exactly what the customer needs—is risky for both the customer and the business.**

As a vegan with severe lactose intolerance, I have become practised at spotting where my own communication with food service staff is most likely to break down. One thing I've learnt is not to assume a dish is vegan unless it's specified. (I once encountered a lovely hummus that, unfortunately for me, contained yoghurt.) Even when a dish is labelled vegan, I usually ask questions to help me assess potential contamination, such as how the item is cooked.

Experience has also taught me that when I ask for milk-free options, I'm often offered lactose-free instead. Lactose-free milk is still cow's milk, which makes it inappropriate for both vegans (that's me) *and* for anyone with a milk protein allergy (not me). However, the everyday person—or the person very newly diagnosed with an allergy or intolerance—often doesn't know the difference between these things. Remember the Curse of Knowledge? The risk of miscommunication can be increased when you are working across different cultures, because terminology, certifications or labelling may be different, or things are simply lost in translation.

These misunderstandings are real and need to be addressed. But in my experience, ***the biggest challenge is contamination.*** A kitchen can get extremely busy, and some people underestimate the severity of possible consequences from contamination. Or they may assume they're dealing with an allegedy instead of an allergy. Or the customer fails to mention their allergy (or intolerance) because they have assumed the item is safe. **Always** prompt customers to ask or tell you about allergies.

It is never a good idea to guess how "real" or "severe" the customer's allergy is. Strictly uphold the food safety procedures and deliver excellent customer service.

> **Felicia Middleton, US—author, food service design consultant, Foodie Builder at Urban Aesthetics**
> *I have a lot of allergies. I'm not going to die if I eat a nut, but I will be sick. I have been in positions where I have gotten sick in restaurants. I know they are taught what to do, that they are supposed to separate and completely wash anything that touches an allergen, but they don't always do that. I think more extensive training is needed.*

Because mistakes and miscommunication happen, I recommend all food service businesses have a robust complaints procedure in place. If you make it easy for people to contact you with concerns or bad experiences (from general customer service to suspected food poisoning to allergic reactions), you can potentially find the fault in the system early enough to prevent a major incident. Handle it well, and you might also divert people from complaining to the food inspectors, or worse, the press.

Always be empathetic to anyone who thinks you have caused them harm or risked their life. It's both good customer service and basic human decency.

A sobering fact about allergies and inclusion

The age group at highest risk of death from an allergic reaction is youth aged 16–24. This age group is transitioning from being taken care of by a parent to being responsible for their own choices. They may not have the experience to know how a commercial kitchen works, and they may lack the confidence to speak up about what they can and cannot eat.

This age group is also very focused on belonging. Often, they don't disclose their allergies when eating with friends because they don't want to be seen as "difficult" or "dramatic". Eating out, especially with others, is supposed to be fun and uncomplicated.

As a group, this age bracket is more likely to take risks and make assumptions. Together, the Food Standards Agency and Allergy UK have created an EasyToAsk Campaign to change this behaviour, specifically because it's *not* easy to ask. It's often awkward, embarrassing, inconvenient or prone to mistakes.

What you can do: Invite people to ask for options and to request more information about ingredients. Put that invitation on your menus, on your website, on signage inside the business. Train hosts or servers to ask whether anyone has specific allergies or dietary preferences to ensure customers can be guided to appropriate options and information.

Don't wait for your customers to gather the courage to ask. Invite them to ask, as often and clearly as you can.

It can save lives.

Caron Pollard, UK—allergy mum and digital marketing expert, co-founder of Teal App
"My daughter's allergies include dairy, egg, nuts and fish. She experienced her first anaphylaxis a year ago after in-

gesting milk accidentally while abroad—this was a poignant moment in our life that revealed how we need to protect her future. She now carries adrenaline auto-injector pens with her to protect her from serious reactions in the future.

It is very common to have a fragmented and long-winded journey to diagnosis and management with reliance on limited offline touchpoints for support. Like many others, we have spent a lot of time on "Dr Google" and social media, which may not always provide qualified or correct information.

My daughter will go out in the world one day, and I want her to be prepared with all the resources needed to live her life safely."

Takeaways

- If someone tells you they have an allergy, take it seriously.
- Allergies are difficult to quantify, diagnose, treat or cure.
- People can have multiple allergies.
- You don't have to understand immunology. You do have to understand and prevent contamination of food.

Free Resources

A colour pdf for a Teal App poster to display in your food outlets is available at **teal.heatherlandex.com**

Further links to statistics, campaigns and free resources are available at **freeresources.heatherlandex.com**

Chapter 9

Religious Diets

In this chapter:
How religion shapes diet
What food service can do
Halal (Islam)
Kosher (Judaism)
(Other religions are discussed briefly at
bonuschapter.heatherlandex.com)

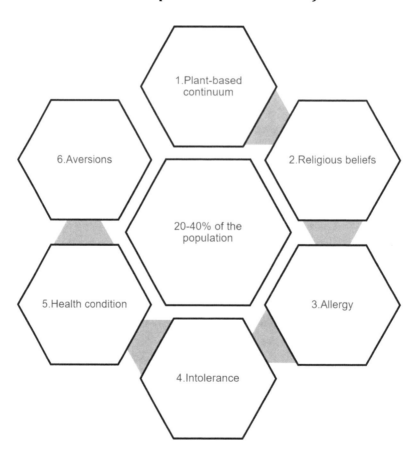

1. Plant-based continuum

2. Religious beliefs

3. Allergy

4. Intolerance

5. Health condition

6. Aversions

20-40% of the population

9.1 How religion shapes diet

Many religions and cultures have rules about food. For example, depending on where you are in the world, anywhere from 5–30% of the population are vegetarian. Those regional differences correlate to an extent with religion, especially on the extreme ends of the scale. Take the high end of 30%. That's the rate of vegetarianism in India, where many Hindus, Jains and Sikhs follow vegetarian diets. However, not all followers of a particular faith have identical dietary preferences. Religious dietary needs and preferences will vary among individuals depending in part on their level of ***observance***, or strictness.

It is a gradient.

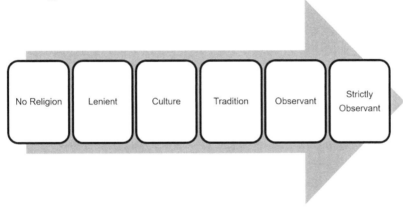

This gradient diagram is overly simplified, but I hope it clarifies that many people are born into a culture that has been shaped by religion, even if they are not observant followers of that religion. To take a non-food example: I am not religious, but I still celebrate Christmas as part of my cultural tradition.

Because of the overlap between religion and culture, even people that call themselves non-religious may follow some food-related rules or traditions that they were brought up with, either consistently or in certain settings (e.g., in their home communities or when they are with family).

9.2 What this means for food service

It means you need to look at your local population before you can develop a plan about how to reach and serve customers with religious dietary preferences.

According to World Population View 2021, 24% of the global population follow Islam. However, that statistic is not the same across regions. In the UK only 6% of the population follow Islam. In Nigeria that figure is 50%. It's 5% in Denmark, 1% in the US, 14% in India and 99% in Algeria.
The number of followers of any given religion in your area will vary. And I don't just mean from one country to the next.

The Muslim population in an urban centre on the east coast of the US is likely to be quite a bit larger than it is in a small town in Alaska. You can likely find information relevant to your local population from your city council, religious communities, government-issued publications or census results. If you are not sure where to start, your local librarians are a good choice. Librarians are extensively trained in both finding data and helping others find it.

If your business is located particularly close to churches, mosques or religious-oriented institutions (such as schools), add that into your considerations. There are also times of the year where plant-based specials may be more popular, such as Chinese New Year, Lent or other religious holidays.

> **Note**
> Businesses relying heavily on international tourism typical-
> ly need to be even more inclusive to remain competitive, as
> they are more likely to receive people—including large tour
> groups—from diverse religious and cultural backgrounds.
> The rest of this chapter is aimed at understanding halal
> and kosher claims. Islam and Judaism are far from the only
> two religions in the world, but they are both detailed in
> **Codex Alimentarius,** an international set of standards cre-
> ated by the UN Food and Agriculture Organization and the
> World Health Organization to aid fair trade and food safety.
> Therefore, halal and kosher claims have to follow rules set
> out by religious or ritual authorities.
> I myself am not religious, and my understanding of what
> it means to truly include these groups is still evolving. As
> a result, I have tried not to give too many of my own opin-
> ions in this chapter. Instead, I posed questions to observant
> followers of Islam and Judaism and related their answers
> here to help readers consider how they might become more
> inclusive in this area.

9.3 Halal (Islamic)

*"An estimated 70% of all Muslims globally do adhere to at least
some of the restrictions associated with halal foods."*
—H. Al-Mazeedi et al., 2013

**Q: What is halal, and does it include more than just the spe-
cific methods of slaughtering animals for meat?**

> **A: Saadia Faruqi, US—author and interfaith activist**
> *Halal means lawful or allowed, and it is defined in contrast to
> haram, which is the unlawful or forbidden. Anything can be ha-
> lal or not. It's not only food, it's anything our religious scripture*

says is good, including being a good person, telling the truth, prayer.

There are only four or five things involved in halal food.

No pork, no blood, no meat from animals that died of other causes. *Nothing on which the name of any other god has been pronounced, which might happen if someone from another religious tradition were to prepare the meal.*

The other aspect of food that is important is how meat is slaughtered, which is called zabiha. There are strict regulations about how meat is slaughtered in Islam, which is not the same as halal. Halal is what is allowed, zabiha is how it is prepared.

When an animal is slaughtered according to zabiha, a prayer is said, and they have to be away from other animals so other animals don't see the slaughter. A very sharp knife is used, and the blood must be allowed to drain out. In most meat plants in the US, they kill the animals by other means, such as electricity. So that meat might be halal because it's not pig or already-dead animal, but it would not be zabiha.

Muslims fall along a spectrum of how religious or observant they are—not everyone is the same. Some people only follow halal, others follow halal and zabiha, and others follow neither. Dairy and eggs don't come into it.

Q: Would a vegan restaurant or meal be a good option for a practicing Muslim?

A: Saadia Faruqi, US—author and interfaith activist

I wouldn't necessarily go into a vegan restaurant. Actually, I guess I would, but I myself follow halal not zabiha because I live in the US. I can follow halal easily, but I cannot check how the animal is slaughtered.

But because a prayer should be said during slaughter, a lot of Muslims don't eat meat when they eat out. They want a vegetarian or vegan option to avoid eating meat at all. My husband is so strict in what he wants to eat that if he orders a vegetarian pizza, he will ask the pizza person not to cut the pizza,

> *because, in his mind, they may have used the same knife to cut a pepperoni pizza just before. He is also a vegetarian; it's not just religious for him.*

According to the *Codex Alimentarius* guidelines, "halal food can be prepared, processed or stored in different sections or lines within the same premises where non-halal foods are produced, provided that necessary measures are taken to prevent any contact between halal and non-halal foods." However, many restaurants are unaware of these restrictions, as Muhammed Asif's experiences show below.

> **Muhammad Asif, UK–CEO of Main Course Associates**
> *I generally ask only one question, and it is something people generally cannot answer or often get wrong. If the ingredient is halal, whether it's meat or fish, I ask if the preparation is halal. They don't know.*
> *I went into a place and asked them whether their meat was halal. They said it was.*
> *"Is the preparation halal?" I asked.*
> *"Yeah."*
> *So I asked, "How is the fish prepared?"*
> *"We put it in the batter and stuff then whack it in the oven."*
> *"What other things are in the oven?"*
> *And she said that on the top rack, they had pork and other meat.*
> *I said, "THAT'S NOT HALAL."*
> *She said, "But look, we have certification."*

Q: What does serving halal mean in practice? How have your customers responded to the procedures you have in place to be able to serve halal?

> **A: Khalid Latif, US—New York University, Chaplin; director of NYUs Islamic Centre; owner of Honest Chops and Burgers by Honest Chops Restaurant**
> *Years ago, HSBC [a global bank and the largest bank in Eu-*

rope] valued the global halal market to be in the trillions.

Halal preparation is not limited to meat.... There might be substances that are problematized: alcohol, gelatin, rennet in cheeses. You can find something to eat in most places, but you might need a conversation with people on the preparation of it.

In our halal dining hall, we have two full-time supervisors that are there the entire day. We also used an external certifying agency. So, people walk in and say, "We are eating here because we know you and we know we can trust what you are feeding us."

When someone who observes halal goes to a restaurant, they might ask the person there to cook their meal in a separate pan or on a different grill so there's not cross-contamination. For the most part, people are pretty receptive to that.

Experts' opinions about the demand for halal catering

When I worked at the London Olympic Games 2012, there was a whole line for halal preparation that included three separate refrigerated kitchens dedicated to preparing only halal. Even the trolleys transporting foods from fridges to the restaurants were colour coded. This is when I learned how important halal separation is to the consumer. I was impressed with the effort taken to guarantee that halal standards were upheld.

Fran Collison, UK—safety director

A predominant amount of meat in the UK is halal. All NZ meat is halal. The 2012 Olympics had a dedicated halal fridge [line of prep fridges].

Jacqui McPeake, UK—owner of JACS Ltd. and former head of catering at a large university

Some will accept our word that we serve halal meat, while others want to see the packaging or stamp of authenticity.

There was a student society within the university [where I used to work] and sometimes they would come and speak to the chef so they could reassure their students that we were serving halal.

> *I think a lot of the UK does have halal meats but does not advertise it. If your customer wants halal meats, advertise it!*
>
> *There can be negative pushback, though. In one of our areas, some of our students were against the principles of halal slaughter, although they ate meat. We had to offer two different meat dishes, one halal and one not, which was complicated. You have to know your customer, but that's always true. And you have to be upfront and honest.*

9.4 Kosher (Jewish)

Keeping kosher (following the laws of kashrut) means strict product separation during storage, cooking and serving. One set of utensils and equipment is used for meat and another set is used for dairy. Dairy and meat should not be eaten together; there should be a time gap in between. In a kosher home there are likely two sets of dishes, cookware, crockery and cutlery, etc.

What this means for food service

In catering, there has to be ***complete separation*** of equipment and storage. The website for KLDB, Europe's largest kosher certification agency, explains more:

For a product to be kosher certified, and to qualify for a kosher certificate, each ingredient, food additive and processing aid used in its production must also be kosher. Additionally...the production process must be suitable for kosher requirements and therefore it must be approved by a kosher auditor. Products may be rendered non-kosher if their production lines and equipment are also used to manufacture non-kosher products.

*Food that does not contain any meat or dairy ingredients is known as **parev**. For a food to be kosher certified as parev, it must also not share production equipment with meat or dairy products when these are produced at a temperature above 40°C. Parev foods may include egg and fish.*

On the whole, parev foods present fewer kosher complexities than either meat or dairy foods.

Q: Is kosher too complex to attempt in a non-specialised food outlet?

Fran Collison, UK—safety director
Kosher cannot really be done unless you are a kosher restaurant. At the Olympics 2012, kosher food was bought in.

Jacqui McPeake, UK—owner of JACS Ltd. and former head of catering at a large university
We couldn't offer kosher. It's a really tricky area. We had regular guests that needed kosher, but we couldn't provide that. We had to buy it from a recognized kosher supplier. It came in sealed and we stored it sealed.

Q: Because of the emphasis on the separation of meat and dairy in keeping kosher, would a vegan restaurant be an option for those keeping kosher?

A: Daniella Levy, Israel—author of *Letters to Josep: An Introduction to Judaism*
There is a large spectrum of observance. I think some people who consider themselves to keep kosher would feel comfortable at a restaurant that was completely vegan or vegetarian and some would not. It depends on how they feel about the dietary laws, how much leniency they feel comfortable with.

For example, my parents would probably feel perfectly comfortable, especially if it were a strict vegan restaurant and they knew that there would not be any cross-contamination with anything. There is an issue with vegetables that we have to check for bugs, but there are ways around that because it's certain kinds of vegetables and very easy to check. You could just glance at the plate.

For me personally, it would really depend on the situation. It's important to know that for those of us who are keeping strict kosher, the laws are more complicated than you could possibly imagine. There is also an aspect that even some people who keep kosher are not really aware of, which is the rules surrounding strong flavours. So, onions, garlic, lemons. If a knife is used to cut those things, then that's considered a transfer of flavour just like heat. So, it does get complicated.

It's not something that can be learned in a few days. It can take months to get used to. And even then, we consult experts like the rabbis, who learned these laws in depth. It is very, very complicated and I think it's important for food establishments to know that if they want to cater to people who keep kosher, they would need to work with a kosher supervision company that knows all the rules and how to adapt the kitchen.

What I do know is that if food arrives at the business kosher certified, steps must be taken to ensure it remains kosher, which necessitates strict protocols around the utensils and crockery. This goes way beyond food safety standards, and it's a subject I intend to learn more about. Even I can continue to expand my understanding of inclusivity.

If you'd also like to explore more, check out the bibliography.

Takeaways

● Do you need to know—is it even possible to know—the detailed religious and non-religious beliefs of your individual customers before you will offer to serve them?
● There is more to halal and kosher foods than a claim on a label.
● Never label anything "halal" or "kosher" without understanding the requirements in Codex Alimentarius.
● A vegan option might be acceptable for some on religiously motivated diets, if you can guarantee no animal product contamination.

Free Resources

Links to more resources can be found at **freeresources.heatherlandex.com**

A section of the bonus chapter at **bonuschapter.heatherlandex.com** is dedicated to other religions, including Buddhism, Jainism, Hinduism and Christianity.

Chapter 10

The Plant-based Continuum

In this chapter:
The expanding market
Terminology
Motivations
What food service can do

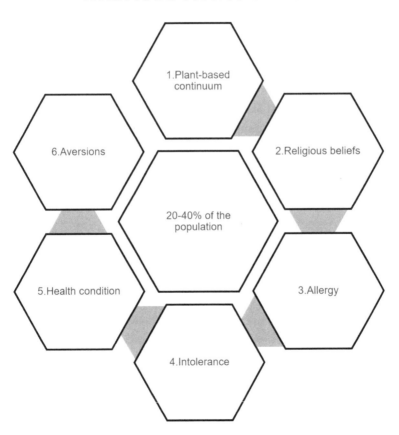

10.1 How many people avoid animal products?

This market is ***exploding***.

🔖 ***55% of people in the UK are reducing their household's meat intake*** (UK Agriculture and Horticulture Development Board, November 2020).

🔖 **7.2 million British adults (out of a total population just over 66 million) currently follow a meat-free diet, and a total of 13 million plan to be meat-free by the end of the year** (Finder UK, January 2021). More than 10% of the UK population is currently vegetarian!

🔖 **An estimated 8% of the world population are vegetarian**, but, as described in Chapter 9, that figure varies regionally (for example, 12% in Denmark but 30% in India). Check your own stats to as local a level as possible, and do not look backwards more than a year or two.

Freeresources.heatherlandex.com has some additional resources for looking up market research on the estimated number of vegans and vegetarians. You can even do your own local market research—even low-tech, cowboy research via surveys and polls on social media may give surprising insights.

Globally, we're seeing a plant-based revolution.

The big companies have seen the trend and are getting into the race. McDonald's and Burger King have both launched burgers with plant-based patties. In 2019, Tyson Foods, the US's leading meat and poultry processing company, launched a plant-based range under the new brand name Raised and Rooted. Arla Foods, the world's fifth-largest dairy company, launched their plant-based JÖRD as a separate brand in March 2020.

Thanks to viral documentaries like *Forks Over Knives* (about disease and diet) or *Game Changers* (where athletes reported better results on a plant-based diet), *The Economist* called 2019 "The Year of the Vegan". In turn, many considered 2020 the "Year of the Flexitarian" (though I think of it as the "Year of the Meat-Reducer"). Food service businesses that do not make efforts to include this exponentially growing market are going to leave a lot of money on the table. Remember—the Common Denominator Effect means that it's not just the increasing numbers of vegans, plant-based eaters and vegetarians that businesses will lose by not offering an inclusive menu. It's everyone else at their table, too.

10.2 Understanding the terms

More and more people are reducing their consumption of animal products. That part is clear. What is less clear for many is how to make sense of the various terms used for those who have cut down on or eliminated animal products. Unfortunately, a great deal of variation exists in how terms are used, both individually and also regionally or culturally. Moreover, some people don't fit neatly into one category; their diet may change in certain settings, as we also saw in the discussion of religious dietary preferences.

In food service, though, you need to know what foods are appropriate for your customer, so I've put together a working frame using definitions from relevant organizations where applicable.

It's a gradient (yes, again!).

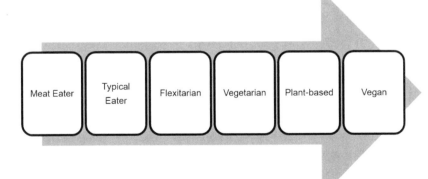

● **Meat-eater** is my term for those who typically eat meat with every meal, consuming more than the average/recommended amount of meat

🍂 **Typical eaters** eat a diverse, omnivorous diet; this is how I characterize the majority group

🍂 **Flexitarians** (sometimes called reducetarians or meat-reducers) eat mostly vegetarian or vegan but occasionally consume meat or fish

🍂 **Vegetarians**, according to the UK Vegetarian Society, do not eat meat, fish or products of slaughter (i.e., animal products which involve killing the animal, like gelatine), but they may eat other products from animals (e.g., eggs or dairy)

🍂 **Plant-based** may be the term whose intended meaning varies the most from person to person. According to the BRCGS' (Brand Reputation Compliance Global Standards) Plant-Based Global Standard, plant-based products are made from plants: they do not intentionally contain materials of animal origin at any stage during production or processing. However, **when used without this formal certification,** the term "plant-based" is not legally restricted. It may be used by businesses and individuals alike to refer to products and diets ranging from "flexitarian" to "mostly (but not entirely) plants" to "basically vegan (minus the ethical aspects)". Commercially, particularly in fast foods, "plant-based" often means meat has been exchanged for a meat substitute which may or may not also be vegan (by virtue of its ingredients, processing and/or preparation). At the other end of the plant-based spectrum is the whole foods plant-based (WFPB) diet, which is a minimally processed diet (e.g., whole grains instead of flours, no refined sugars) that is free of animal products.

🍂 **Vegan** diets also avoid products/ingredients of animal origin (e.g., meat, but also honey) and animal-derived processing aids (e.g., white sugar bleached with bone char; wine clarified with isinglass, which is derived from the swim bladders of fish). A vegan diet that *also* avoids processed foods may overlap significantly with a WFPB diet, but products called "plant-based" by marketers ***should not be assumed to be vegan.*** According to the Vegan Society UK, veganism is not just a diet; it is also "a philosophy and way of living which seeks to exclude—as far as is possible and practicable—all forms of exploitation of, and cruelty to,

96

animals for food, clothing or any other purpose". What is "practicable" is somewhat open to interpretation and dependent on the individual. It is difficult to live a fully vegan lifestyle in modern society, and vegans are on their own continuum of ethical observance. New vegans often start with a basic vegan diet and then move further into the **ethical vegan lifestyle.**

The list above is a starting point, but *each group should be seen as its own continuum within the larger plant-based continuum*. There is a continuum of what it means to be consciously reducing meat intake. There is also a continuum of what it means to be plant-based, vegetarian or vegan. Someone who calls themselves vegetarian may eat fish (or in some cases even chicken), because they associate "meat" with red meat only. Someone else who identifies as vegetarian may be unpleasantly surprised if the "vegetarian" meal provided for them by the caterer is salmon or a cheese containing rennet[4]. A flexitarian may be fully vegan at home but eat whatever is served at friends' dinner parties. A Sikh individual may follow a vegetarian diet that includes milk products but not eggs. Meanwhile, an otherwise strict vegan woman may allow honey or eat eggs from hens she raises herself—but don't assume she does.

Although specialized terms exist for pretty much any diet you can imagine that reduces or eliminates animal products (e.g., pescatarian, ovo-lacto vegetarian, reducetarian and more—see Glossary for details), in practice, *you don't need a box for every person to provide a great customer service experience.* For example, if someone tells you they want a vegetarian option, assume that means the description of vegetarian offered by the Vegetarian Society above, and then accept alternative meanings if the customer provides them. If that customer orders the vegetable Pad Thai, make sure they know that there's, say, a bit of fish sauce in the packaged sauce used to make it, but don't argue with

---

4   *Rennet, typically extracted from the stomach lining of calves, is frequently used to curdle milk in cheese production.*

the customer about the definition of "vegetarian" if they say that's fine. Some people are more flexible with their diets outside the home out of necessity, while others avoid terms (like pescatarian, which is vegetarian plus fish) they think won't be easily understood by the general public. Many factors play into how a person will describe their dietary preferences.

You don't need to decide what the customer wants to eat. That's their job. Your role is to ensure they can make an informed decision about the options you offer. *Know your product and be able to talk about it.*
Regardless of where one is on the plant-based continuum, there is no obligation to be a member of any formal society or follow any rules or definitions. It's also important to know that individuals don't necessarily stay at the same spot on the continuum throughout their lives; instead, they may become more or less plant-based—permanently or temporarily—for a variety of reasons. The overall trend, though, is that more and more people are moving further toward the plant-based and vegan end of the continuum. As you'll see in the next section, what they want out of a plant-based meal tends to change the further along that continuum they are.

10.3 Why people choose the plant-based continuum

> **David Pannel, co-founder of Vegan Business Tribe (vegan marketing experts) in the UK, describes this transformation as "The Vegan Journey".**
> *"Some may start out as plant-based for health reasons, but once they start learning more as they expose themselves to more and more vegan-targeted marketing, social media and products, they may then become vegan due to environmental or animal welfare reasons. They may therefore change their buying habits. They may move from meat substitutes, mimics or alternatives, to more vegetable-based products that no longer resemble meat."*

Kayleigh Nicolaou, UK—Kakadu Creative - A Different Design Agency | Ethical, Sustainable & Vegan

I think that the market growth we're seeing is phenomenal. And that's what has given us the confidence to shout a bit more about our personal ethics and our ethos within the business.

Some people say you have to call it plant-based, and other people say, "Oh, no, that will confuse people, call it vegan." In reality, it doesn't matter. It's a vegan revolution and it's a plant-based revolution, both at the same time. What I've been finding is that a lot of people don't even know the difference.

Claire Smith, UK—vegan entrepreneur and investor, co-founder of Beyond Animal

I see a clear trend towards veganism, but with the terminology "plant-based". It's been helpful for some people to feel they could adopt a diet without justifying a heavy moral philosophy to their friends.

People generally choose the plant-based continuum for one or more of the following reasons:
- health concerns (e.g., as part of a diet aimed at improving or preventing a specific medical condition)
- environmental interests
- ethical or religious motivations

We are living in an age where information is available within seconds. People are looking to improve their health, help protect the environment, prevent animal suffering and so on. To many people, vegan, vegetarian or flexitarian diets seem like an effective, achievable way to do that, particularly when the focus is on fresh, minimally processed ingredients. **The world is changing, and the expectation is that you will change too.**

In his 2017 book *How Not to Die*, Dr Michael Gregor (MD) summarized what an increasing number of researchers, nutritionists and ordinary people have come to believe: "It turns out a more plant-based diet may help prevent, treat, or reverse every single one of our fifteen leading causes of death [in the US]." That belief is reflected in the growing demand for plant-based products.

> **Santi Aliaga, Spain—CEO of Zyrcular Foods, plant-based alternatives producer**
> *Our approach is to identify trends for the following years regarding protein. Plant-based products and plant-based technology—it's a reality right now, it's booming. We need to be open to new knowledge or new proposals worldwide and identify new sources of plant-based protein that are local.*
>
> *Consumers every year are much better informed about how the food they are eating is made. So you have to be very transparent these days. New generations are looking for a new pattern of consumption quite different to our parents' and grandparents'.*

Claire Williams, a senior programme manager at a large environmental charity, said she has noticed a large percentage of vegans and vegetarians within environmental protection. In her view, **food is at the heart of many environmental issues because of its contribution to climate change and global biodiversity loss.** When her organization eats out together at functions, team building events or holiday parties, she says they choose a place with multiple good vegan and vegetarian options, adding that many environmental charities have vegetarian policies for when they organize in-house catering, events and conferences.

This emphasis on the link between diet and environment is not limited to those working specifically in environmental protection efforts. Environmental concerns have become increasingly mainstream, especially among younger generations, and they are driving a significant portion of dietary changes.

> **Henrik Saxe is the director of Mindful FOOD Solutions** and formerly a professor at the Danish Technical University (DTU), Copenhagen University (KU) and the University of Southern

Denmark (SDU). He works mostly with the life cycle assessment of food and has worked on projects including the New Nordic Diet and the Eldorado Project. I spoke to him for his thoughts on the increasing influence of environmental concerns on dietary preferences.

He said, *"The simple rule of thumb which I guess everybody knows—it's not a big surprise—is to avoid beef. That's the most important recommendation. That'll take away 80% of the climate impact."*

I couldn't help myself from making a joke about cow farts and belches (which produce methane gas, which is a greenhouse gas twenty-eight times more potent than carbon dioxide in contributing to climate change), but Henrik clarified seriously that methane is just one aspect of the problem. The other key issue is the clearing of rain forest in South America to grow feed for the cattle industry. Before a cow winds up on someone's plate, it must first consume 50-250 times its body weight in feed. And because Europe imports about two-thirds of its protein, European beef consumption impacts rain forest destruction in South America.

To my surprise, Henrik explained that when it comes to climate change, the ingredients in one's food matter more than how far that food has travelled.

"There are a few misconceptions," he said, "usually because the journalists have been telling people this is a major problem for decades. I think that transport, if it comes [to Europe] from South America, that's really bad. Or if it's got plastic packaging or something like that, which is a separate problem. But it's minor in terms of the climate change that we are experiencing right now and in the future. So what I usually tell people is to please focus on what's most important: what's on your plate. It's not really where it comes from. It's the ingredients. Cut down on or avoid beef, cut down on meat—and fish as well, for biodiversity reasons."

If you are wondering why Henrik mentions fish and biodiversity, it is because even "sustainable fishing" results in bycatch.

According to the website for the Food and Agriculture Organisation of the United Nations, "Bycatch is often composed of juveniles of targeted species, small or low-value fish, or accidently caught sea turtles, rays or sharks, some of which are endangered species. Whatever is not kept for use is thrown back into the sea dead or dying and is considered discard, another harmful practice for our species and environment."

As Henrik's, Claire's and Santi's words show, the reasons motivating people to reduce meat and step onto the plant-based continuum are not going away. If anything, these factors will motivate even more people to reduce meat in the coming years.

10.4 What this means for food service

First of all, it means there are *a lot of people interested in plant-based options.* Not only will that number continue to grow, but more and more people already on the plant-based continuum are likely to be moving away from highly processed meat substitutes and, increasingly, toward fresh, environmentally friendly, whole food plant-based options.

Only a very small percentage of vegans and vegetarians eat exclusively at dedicated vegan or vegetarian restaurants. The vast majority of those on the plant-based continuum are happy to go to any restaurant where they can get excellent food and service at a fair price. *If you can deliver that to them (and you make sure they know you can!) they will be happy to spend their money with you.*

My recommendation: Find the Common Denominator on the continuum, and work from there. In this case, that's the vegan option.

A vegan option is guaranteed to be vegetarian, but a vegetarian option is not guaranteed to be vegan.
A vegan option is guaranteed to be plant-based, but a plant-based option is not guaranteed to be vegan.
Vegan is not just a vegetarian who doesn't eat eggs or milk, although that might be the simple way to explain the diet to someone who has never heard of it. Because animal products

can "hide" in places like colourings (e.g., Natural Red 4, derived from insects), beverages (filtering processes for beer or wine that depend on isinglass or egg whites) or E numbers (additives, preservatives and stabilisers), access to truly vegan food—not just "food made from plant ingredients"—is often difficult.

To complicate matters, there is currently no legal standard for labelling items as suitable for vegetarians and vegans. ***It is expected that food labelled vegan is free from animal ingredients and processing aids,*** but in terms of contamination, there is no maximum limit of what is allowed.

This confusion is a big reason for businesses to make their inclusive options from scratch and keep them simple (yet colourful and tasty). That way you don't have to guarantee and test the entire food chain or prove a "free-from" claim. If you can manage your supplier information and ingredients, and you have a written allergy matrix or list to refer to, you can give the information to your customers. Your transparency and communication may win their loyalty, since many places are primarily targeting the meat reducers and flexitarians (a big part of that 55% of the UK population mentioned earlier) and are not necessarily interested in meeting the needs of vegans, allergy sufferers or anyone outside "the mainstream". Some big fast-food chains have taken the approach that a plant-based option means swapping the meat patty on a burger for a plant-based substitute...never mind the cheese and mayonnaise on top, nor the fact it was prepared on the same equipment as the beef burgers. (More on that in Chapter 13.)

Cindy Willcocks, UK—founder of Arterne CIC and the L.O.V.E Leadership Academy
At a few places, I've said I'm vegan and they kind of look at me. And I say, "Nothing animal related, no dairy products, no meat." Then they say, "Is that because of allergy or just a preference?" And my instinct is to say, "Does that matter?"

There is a demand for **clean vegan options, treated with the care typically reserved for customers with severe allergies:**

supplied, prepared and cooked without contamination. It's a newer idea, because it is more difficult to do, but that also means it could be why customers eat with you and not elsewhere. It's a unique selling point to offer plant-based options without any "may contain" or "traces of" labels. Remember: get the Common Denominators excited about you, and you will capture their business, the business of those dining with them and the business of others in their networks.

If the biggest potential issue is contamination, the biggest potential USP is a *clean vegan option*.
But remember: **only promise what you are committed to delivering, and always be honest.**

Takeaways
- Nobody fits perfectly into a box. People exist on continuums within the plant-based continuum.
- Accept the definitions are only a guideline; individuals make their own choices.
- Vegetarian is not necessarily vegan; vegan is vegetarian.
- Plant-based is not necessarily vegan; vegan is plant-based.
- **ALWAYS BE HONEST.**

Free Resources

For links to more statistics, campaigns or free resources go to
freeresources.heatherlandex.com

A bonus chapter looking more deeply at this subject is available
at **bonuschapter.heatherlandex.com**

Chapter 11

An Inclusive Solution: The Clean Vegan Option

In this chapter:
One new option = many solutions

By now, your head may be buzzing with the potential complications of inclusion. There is so much to be aware of when considering safety, liability and feasibility.

I understand. But remember, you don't need to strive to be 100% inclusive to every imaginable dietary preference on Day One. **Be as inclusive as possible, given your specific resources and circumstances, to increase your capacity and capabilities in the long term.**

My goal in writing this book—and hopefully your goal in reading it—is to *find a relatively straightforward, achievable way for you to attract and keep the biggest possible slice of the customers you are currently missing out on.*

11.1 Finding the overlap

First things first: before you attempt to be more inclusive, you must evaluate your *food safety and allergy management systems.* Once they are robust and functioning well, a *huge benefit can be gained by considering adding a customizable option with a clean vegan base.*

Why vegan? Vegan options, done well, appeal to more than just vegans.

● Some of those with religious dietary preferences are drawn to options that simplify the decision-making process by ensuring that slaughter methods or certain animal-derived ingredients (including milk and some meats) are a non-issue.

● Vegan options can also be a popular choice among vegetarians, flexitarians and everyone else in that 55% of the population reducing meat consumption (UK).

● A ***clean*** (details below) vegan option can serve those with food allergies and/or intolerances to any (or many) of the major animal-based allergens: milk, egg, fish or shellfish. They are also appropriate for individuals with alpha-gal syndrome/allergy[5] or lactose intolerance. (Remember the 23% of the UK population that avoid milk?)

Why "clean"? "Clean" here means that processes are in place and followed to ensure no contamination during preparation or serving of the base dish. As a result, there is no trace of any meat, dairy or fish in the food, which can be a unique selling point to the groups detailed above. (See Chapter 14 for ideas on how to effectively communicate this information.)

> **Loui Blake, UK—plant-based investor, restaurant entrepreneur and speaker**
> *I've opened a number of plant-based restaurants, kitchens and a pub, including the UK's largest fully vegan restaurant.*
>
> *We actually did a small survey last Christmas at one of the restaurants. I wanted to understand just what percentage of customers weren't vegan. Obviously, we're a 100% vegan*

---

5   *According to the American Academy of Allergy, Asthma and Immunology, alpha-gal allergy is a food allergy to a carbohydrate molecule called galactose-alpha-1,3-galactose, found in most mammalian or "red" meat. The syndrome is linked to bites from certain ticks. Symptoms can be severe, including life-threatening anaphylaxis. Unlike most food allergies, reactions can be delayed 3-8 hours after ingestion.*

> *restaurant. We did four very simple questions, multiple choice. For example, "I am vegan/vegetarian/flexitarian/meat-eater." I was incredibly surprised. We found **that over 80% of our customers weren't vegan. Eighty per cent, which was really interesting.***

In other words, **the viable market for a clean vegan option far exceeds the number of vegans.**

Why customizable? With this approach, you aren't just adding a menu option for a specific group; you're adding a menu option for all your customers. *As long as the vegan base is guaranteed free from animal products and prepared separately,* you can offer the option to add egg, a vegan protein like tofu or tempeh, or even a cheesy meaty version. It's a way to please everyone, and it justifies flexible pricing.

Will people be scared off by a "clean vegan option"?

You don't have to call it that. You definitely want people to know it's there, and you want to ensure the groups who will be most excited about it can find it, but people like good food. *This dish can be an additional option for all customers,* and choice is valuable on a menu. Before I became vegan or even vegetarian, I ate "green options" because I like green food. Plus, vegetables are often colourful, and I am one of those people who likes to try something different each time I eat out. I even like variety within the same dish and have never been a fan of risotto or pasta dishes because I get bored halfway through.

Remember, however, that new customers won't automatically start flocking to you the second you add this to your menu. They may not be in your current customer base. You need to shout about your efforts, communicate them on your website, menu, everywhere! Speak directly to Common Denominators and tell them what you are offering them. *If you do it well, these efforts can continue to grow your customer base indefinitely.*

An option that meets the needs of many groups is an excellent place to start. But inclusivity is a process, not a destination. From here, you can continue to regularly revisit and improve your capabilities and creativity. As your expertise in serving these markets develops, you improve your options to keep expanding your customer base and generating more excitement and word-of-mouth, organic marketing.

Does inclusivity really make good business sense?
According to Main Course Associates' (MCA) Return on Investment calculator it does! MCA are leading hospitality industry specialists providing financial accounting and management support.

Do keep in mind that the calculator is not intended as specific financial advice for your business and circumstance, but rather as a fun, accessible interactive tool that can help you visualize the potential benefits of inclusivity.

MCA are included in **Author Recommendations** at the back of this book.

Takeaways

🖊 A clean vegan option (guaranteed contamination-free of animal products) can appeal to a significant portion of people with different dietary preferences.

Free Resources

MCA's Inclusivity ROI Calculator is available at
freeresources.heatherlandex.com.

Part 3

Getting to Inclusivity

Stand out from the competition.

Why does inclusivity matter *now*?
In some ways, the pandemic has provided opportunity. Many food service businesses are downsizing or at the very least distracted due to the damage of the past year. Until now, simply surviving has been a competitive advantage. However, the situation has become dire. Smart businesses are seeking ways to navigate a difficult landscape and stay competitive. ***I want to help you make headway by increasing your loyal customer base and growing your business.***

One consequence of the pandemic is that many restaurants have simplified their menus to cope with reduced demand and unpredictable closings. As a result, some places that are usually inclusive have become less so.

In June 2020, after lockdown 1.0, **Muhammed Asif (CEO of Main Course Associates in the UK)** surveyed clients, industry specialists and customers to chart changes in the industry. He summarized some of his key findings for me.
"What has been quite interesting is we've noticed that some of the things that were quite high up on the agenda of customers pre-Covid have actually dropped down a bit. Things like, for example, sustainability, came quite a lot further down the list.

Hygiene was right on the top and rightly so. At the moment, that is really what people want.

Inclusivity was an important point. *Even though businesses will be running a reduced menu at a reduced cost base when they reopen, a lot of customers have said, "We would still like to*

110

> see a vegetarian/vegan option on the menu. Don't remove that."
>
> **Restaurant owners 100% need to be thinking about inclusivity, how to bring it in. Once they start thinking about it, it helps them. It's not a hindrance—it's a way to actually increase and grow their profits.**
>
> *If they continue to see veganism [and other dietary preferences] as a hindrance, it's going to be a problem for them. Accept it and embrace it and become inclusive. I think they will see it. Their turnover will increase."*

Developing your ability to be inclusive is especially valuable in this "new normal". **Niche businesses are closing**, because they rely on people's willingness to travel. The prestigious Vanilla Black vegan restaurant in London is one example. Other restaurants that specialize in serving those with dietary preferences are also suffering, and many of them will not survive. During the industry recovery period, I expect there to be immense opportunities for other businesses to capture those customers if they are willing to put in the work to get inclusivity right.

Regardless of whether you want to attract new customers, *it's important to consider that even your current customer base is likely to come back changed after the pandemic.* Many people have a renewed focus on their personal health, and the interest in fresh, healthy, plant-based options as a means of improving health is likely to accelerate, including among your established customers.

> **Mark McCulloch, UK—CEO and founder of Supersonic Inc., a brand and marketing consultancy**
>
> *There is a huge opportunity there. If there was ever a time to reinvent your business, be agile and think about things in a different way, it's now. An awful lot of people will have rethought how they live their lives, what they do and how they can live longer. Our mortality is in question.*
>
> **The time is now.**

If you upsize, downsize or move to a new location, remember to consider inclusivity potential. Things like the layout of the kitchen, space for separate preparation, equipment to avoid contamination (e.g., a separate fryer, separate grill or easily dividable grill like the SynergyGrill) are much easier to integrate from the start than they are to retrofit.

> **James Lipscombe, CEO and owner of The Chesterford Group** (which operates a large chain of fish and chip shops and restaurants in the UK already catering to vegans and coeliacs) shared his experiences on the value of equipment in assuring a clean vegan option:
>
> *"There are challenges with "may contain traces" disclaimers in a business of our nature. You can probably imagine the challenges we have with pieces of equipment, with different fryers that we use for different products. We rotate cooking oil to ensure that we cook chips to more of a golden colour in slightly older oil that has previously had other products cooked in. It can be operationally really difficult to ensure the products and oil are clear from cross-contamination with meat and fish products. Even when we filter our oil on a daily basis, there will always be (tiny) "traces of" animal products in the oil, particularly of concern to allergy sufferers and vegans.*
>
> *I found a way around this contamination problem by using the SynergyGrill for a vegan burger. The grill can be easily divided and cleaned, and any fat that drips down is carbonised and falls to the bottom. It is good separation from a food safety perspective."*

As an added bonus, James reported that out of his vegan menu options (all marketed from a pro-climate angle), the vegan burger sells best. Maybe his catchment area just really likes a good burger, but maybe he's seeing inclusivity in action: his customers may well prefer the clean vegan option over the options with "traces of meat or animal products" disclaimers.

As you are considering the layout and equipment needs of your business, remember that inclusivity must be built on a foundation of food safety. For example, there are never enough handwashing basins, which either causes staff to cut corners or waste time walking a distance. Prioritize making food safety efficient.

> **Robert Bradley, UK—director at Solar Compliance Ltd. and Learnsafe**
> *A lot of safety goes back to design. If you can design a kitchen from the start, you can develop a strong safety culture. Post-Covid, take any commercial advantage (provided you plan it properly), adapt and survive.*
>
> *If you try to stick to what you've done the last five years, it won't happen. Look at the options, look at the trends and be very adaptable.*

There are other ways to leverage the recent changes in the industry. For example, online menus, QR codes and automated ordering systems have become more common and important. Excitingly, these tools happen to allow for better management of dietary preferences on menus and create valuable opportunities for communication.

> **Dennis Wilson, Canada—founder and rapid sales growth expert at Small Business Dream (a marketing automation tool) and DeliveryBizConnect**
> *"It's not just the people coming to your restaurants [that matter], but also the takeout capabilities. Google AdWords and Facebook ads for those types of things [dietary preferences] would be so cheap, because no one is doing it. You could generate specific online order traffic from that family who is going, "Where is there a freaking coeliac-friendly restaurant?"*
>
> *It is quite neat in today's world that everyone wants to go touchless. You have your online menus, which have the ability to have rich details behind a menu item and far more categories. You are not limited by paper. Just by scanning a QR code at the table, you can see the vegan options, sub-classified to show the peanut-allergy-friendly stuff. You can literally classify your whole menu."*

If you can target new customers' dietary preferences (and with them, their networks), you can bring them into your loyal customer base by positioning yourself as the best, the first or the only business in town to cater to them. A stronger local catchment like this can both help in your post-Covid business recovery now *and* make your business more resilient and profitable so it can weather future crises.

Serving more people makes business sense, whoever they may be. But attracting a higher percentage of the population within a fixed local radius (your takeaway capabilities, for example) is better suited to a new world where catchment areas are more fixed, tourism and travel is down, and where even commuting may slow or stop altogether for periods of time as the tail of the pandemic drags out.

Stand out from the competition. Attract groups.

Some of the possible changes I am suggesting will require significant improvements to your current food safety systems, equipment or training that will not be possible for every business, especially now. But other changes are free or involve minor expenses. By **making the best of what you have**, you create an opportunity to attract and keep customers whose needs aren't being met elsewhere.

Many postponed birthdays and overdue celebrations await the end of the pandemic. A lot of people are very eager to go out and enjoy all the things they haven't been able to. I know I'm keeping a wish list of all the things I'm looking forward to! Sadly, when the world re-opens, many people will find that their favourite restaurants have closed down.

I really hope whilst you are reading this book, we start to see a 2021 boomerang effect for the food service industry. I want to see people returning to public life, to socialising, to cafes and restaurants and pubs and hotels. And I want to see your business finding ways to attract more of those groups so they celebrate with *you*. By catering to dietary preferences, you can bring in those groups who are hungry to be included. They win, and so do you.

114

Takeaways

- Prioritize making food safety efficient.
- Stand out from the competition.
- Attract groups.

*[NB: At the time of writing, the industry is in crisis. I would like to direct you to **Hospitality Action** in Author Resources at the back of the book. Hospitality Action is a charity offering support homeless hospitality workers including financial help, mental health support and much more.]*

Free Resources

Find more from Muhammad Asif, plus tips for restaurants, at
bonuschapter.heatherlandex.com

MCA's Inclusivity ROI calculator can be found at
freeresources.heatherlandex.com

Chapter 12

The First Step is Mindset

In this chapter:

The MAPPS Leading Change Model
Mindset
Alignment
Plans
People Systems

I've said it before in this book: ***change is hard, but often rewarding.***

In this section, I am going to identify the pieces you need to set yourself up for successful change.

Stuart Ewen, partner and co-founder of Mindset Associates, introduced me to the MAPPS model for leading change. Stuart has an interesting background in operations, working in change management in large pub chains and as the head of customer experience.

Below, I've adapted the MAPPS model to the concept of inclusivity.

12.1 MAPPS – Leading Change Model

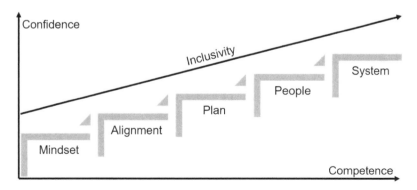

According to the MAPPS model, *mindset* is the first, crucial step toward change. Once you know why you are doing something, your competence increases in correlation with your confidence as you move through the steps needed for transformation.

Each of the steps in the MAPPS model—mindset, alignment, plan, people, systems—must be put in place to boost confidence, improve competence and ultimately achieve greater inclusivity. If you skip or fail a step, you will likely end up back where you started.

12.2 Change Step 1: Mindset

You have to want to become more inclusive. Authentically inclusive, not surface inclusive. You have to care about minority groups' safety and put yourself in their shoes. This first step involves honestly assessing your current level of inclusivity, current food safety standards and your capabilities in allergy management. It means considering what needs to happen to ensure you **do not cause harm,** both in safety management and brand protection terms.

Create a vision of how that looks for your business in your circumstances. How inclusive can you be? How will you communicate and market your inclusivity?

Your reasons for doing this need to be bigger than the money. You must prioritise some of the greater goals discussed in this book: goals of ethical business, sustainable business or future-proof business.

Without that mindset, you limit your success and increase your potential liability. Your team is less likely to understand why you want to change things and less likely to commit to what's needed for change.

> **Robert Bradley, UK—director at Solar Compliance Ltd. and Learnsafe**
> *One of the first lessons in health and safety is to know your limitations. There is so much information to remember, but in the competitive world of hospitality, **there is a danger that***

food business operators want to be able to offer whatever they think the customer will buy without giving sufficient thought to how they can deliver it safely.

One of the main challenges with allergies is the attitudes of chefs and kitchen staff. In many conversations I have had with chefs whilst running training courses and trying to get a serious vegan offer, they often see vegetarians and vegans as being weird, freaks and hippies. It's a massive challenge. Allergy sufferers are sometimes seen as just fussy eaters. Thankfully, on the whole, attitudes appear to be evolving and improving. The positive approach to vegans by some of the leading chefs will further help to improve mindsets."

Examples from the experts

Stuart gave some particularly relevant examples about why having the right mindset is the first step in change management on the MAPPS model. Without the right mindset, neither the customer nor the business experience is a success.

Stuart's example of how mindset affects stock management

What you will find is that when the Ops Manager goes in and talks about stocks, he'll say, "You've written off all those vegan burgers."

The next time, the chef won't order the vegan burger so guess what? He doesn't have to write them off. The chef isn't getting told off for the vegan burgers not being available. He's not getting told that he should have sold those burgers, that maybe he should have tried to put a special on them. He's only getting told off for them being written off.

Stuart's example of how mindset affects planning

"I worked for three months in a Michelin-starred restaurant in the kitchen. If someone vegan or vegetarian showed up, they would make it up on the hoof. Everything else on the menu was properly done and we cooked it fifty times to make sure it was perfect. The poor vegan or whoever it may be would come in and it would literally be, "You'll get what you are given."

In contrast, as Stuart also pointed out, the right mindset leads to success stories.

> **Stuart's example of how mindset affects communication**
> *"I went to Core by Claire Smyth here in London. My dad has a fish allergy. Out came the menu for a fish allergy. They have vegan, vegetarian, fish allergy menus, they have an "I don't want to eat pork" menu. Different options all based around roughly the same ingredients. It was brilliant. I thought they were excellent in terms of what they do."*

It was clear that Stuart's experience at Core was the result of thoughtful planning and communication. Since Core has two Michelin stars, I was intrigued and went to their website. Despite their excellent communication on the menu in the restaurant, there was no mention of dietary preferences on their website. They are missing an opportunity. I have informed them, but received no reply in time for inclusion in this book.

12.3 Change Step 2: Alignment

Alignment of mindset and vision is required when changing anything related to food safety standards. Unless everyone—chefs, servers, marketing specialists, reservation staff, etc.—are involved in and aligned with the goal of inclusivity, you end up with intentional or unintentional sabotage (like the chef in Stuart's first example). Everyone, including all those in part-time, temporary and/or non-specialized roles, should understand why ***inclusivity is a team effort.*** They must know the risks, the opportunities and how their roles can support the vision. **Try to involve your staff in the development of the inclusivity mission and a company culture**. When you do, people will understand why they are being asked to do something extra, you'll gain a diversity of perspectives and creative ideas, and you will uncover challenges or misunderstandings early. All of these benefits will bring you to the *best holistic and practical solution.*

When you give an overview of the important aspects of the new system(s), ensure you translate the vision into actions or tangible things, such as new menus or new scripts/processes for orders. If you have not yet participated in a **food safety culture training,** this is a good time to do so. These trainings are about *being better than the legal requirements* to protect your brand reputation and the safety of your customers.

Ideally, when someone who will require more effort or particular consideration to serve walks into your establishment, staff will be very happy to see them. This customer is one of your best, in terms of potential advocacy. Staff should immediately remember the Common Denominator Effect, the Network Effect and the goodwill extended when typically excluded individuals are enthusiastically welcomed and competently served.

Many corporations have missions and visions, but not all employees know what they are or understand them. When staff are aligned with the mission, each individual understands the concept of inclusivity and the reason behind new procedures or other changes. Staff members are then more likely to diligently follow more complex procedures without cutting corners.

12.4 Change Step 3: Plans

If you begin without a plan, you'll end up with a *false start* that quickly collapses. Consider what it is you are trying to do, and what will help you get there.

During the initial phase of planning, remember to assess what you already have in place. Are your suppliers and food safety management already robust and allergy-friendly, or should you start with improving food safety and the food safety culture? As already mentioned in the **Inclusivity Pyramid,** nearly all businesses are basic-compliant with a **food safety management system.** Fewer have good food safety standards and a **food safety culture.** Very few have **allergy management** or significant awareness of **dietary preferences**. Almost none are targeting people with dietary preferences, often because they are concerned about liability or attracting more "difficult" customers (i.e., those that take more effort to serve). This is where inclusivity becomes very exclusive. Consider where you are on this continuum to judge where you can *realistically begin to improve at this time.*

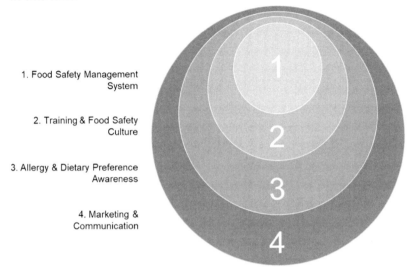

1. Food Safety Management System

2. Training & Food Safety Culture

3. Allergy & Dietary Preference Awareness

4. Marketing & Communication

To become more exclusive, build on food safety as a marketing strategy.

Questions to consider

To make your specific vision of inclusivity a reality, are you going to adapt the menu, alter the ordering process, revise your food safety management system, talk to your suppliers?

Who will need training?

Will you need extra equipment for the back of the house or extra materials such as menus and QR codes for the front of the house?

Do you need to reconsider how online ordering is set up?

What about your signage?

When are you going to launch your new efforts, and how will you advertise them?

Write down those details.

Do you need vegan or allergy specialists to conduct trainings, vegan marketing specialists to help you reach your target group, market researchers to tell you where to focus your efforts? Do you need tech experts, nutritionists, designers, sustainability experts? If you need help connecting with them, I know them all, and my details are at the back of the book and the end of each chapter. Reach out.

12.5 Change Step 4: People

It's necessary to invest time and resources in training your staff to ensure they have the skills they need. You don't want them to end up poorly prepared and stressed out about the possible costs of mistakes.

Keeping your staff highly trained will benefit your business. Ensuring staff understand their job responsibilities and expectations (and limits) and what it means to "do a good job" makes them more likely to stay. You can also reward them for their efforts when you receive a good review or when procedures are followed flawlessly for a period of time. If you acknowledge when their efforts make a difference, they become invested in good outcomes.

Some rewards occur naturally. When ordering procedures become more efficient and more people are happy, servers may feel less time pressure, receive compliments or get tips (where applicable). Support staff through the learning curve so they can enjoy these natural benefits as well.

> **Maria Quereda, Spain—country director for MCA Spain and hospitality operations specialist**
> *When I started to work in hospitality, I liked to drink wine, but I didn't really know anything about it. I was put in front of people and told I should sell £200 bottles of wine. In the beginning I was scared. But as soon as they gave me knowledge and stories, what is behind that wine and what makes it unique, I became the number one seller of wines because I was confident. With knowledge you can do whatever you want.*

> *So, when it comes to chefs, it is exactly the same. If we talk about cross-contamination, of course you need space for proper service, but you also need knowledge. These are the basics of this industry. It's not that the restaurant chefs need to learn it all, but they need to have the right tools and the right information to add that extra service that will bring more revenue."*

12.6 Change Step 5: Systems

Systems are the foundation of inclusivity. Inclusivity relies on an enhanced food safety management system that consists of allergy management, customer service, ordering systems, even marketing and communication systems. It includes onboarding training and signage. It impacts branding, labelling, storage, processes and service.

It takes effort to create the system and all the working parts, but once it is in place, you can operate more efficiently, safely, professionally and prestigiously. You can also operate more flexibly even when staff, menus and chefs change. It is like investing an insurance policy: if an incident or complaint happens, the system is your *due diligence defence*[6] against negligence.

What are some of the systems that will benefit you on the journey toward greater inclusivity?

🕭 **A system to encourage reviews** so that Common Denominators can report your good work to their networks, make word-of-mouth referrals and even submit complaints. Without the feedback and validation this system provides, you and your staff may end up *frustrated or adrift* because you don't know if your efforts are worthwhile, or you are not able to identify faults in the system(s).

---

6   *Risk can never be fully eliminated. However, if someone were to suffer an adverse reaction after eating your food, the documents and evidence you produce in your FSMS/ HACCP would show you took all reasonably practicable steps to reduce risk. The systems you have in place—and the supporting documentation—can establish that you followed the law and were not negligent.*

❧ An ordering system

Maria Quereda, Spain—country director for MCA Spain and hospitality operations specialist

It's not the allergy book but the food book, where you have the whole menu, a small description of the USP of every single plate, the ingredients, allergies and the mise en place. The idea is to give it to every single person working in the restaurants. It doesn't matter if you are the runner or the manager: everyone should be able to answer basic questions on what you have on offer.

❧ A system for labelling to speed up service and reduce mistakes. One simple software tool for labelling and menu creation is allergenchecker.co.uk (see **Author Recommended Resources**). User-friendly, adaptable software means your labels and menus are more likely to be accurate. However, this software does not reduce the need for training or strict separation and cleaning procedures. And remember: any tool is only as good as 1) the data it contains and 2) the person using it.

❧ Signage systems to inform the customer. **Labelling on self-serve buffets** that is consistent, updatable and easy to understand is particularly helpful to all customers. (Be careful with potentially ambiguous icons—more on that in Chapter 14.) Ensure a person with the needed knowledge and skills is available to supervise. Labelling should even extend to the cake on a coffee trolley or the sandwiches at a meeting.

Signage prompting customers to inform you about allergies or intolerances is always a good idea, but make sure you also tell them *how* to inform you. Clear communication processes reduce risk, increase efficiency and help customers feel more confident visiting you. Even those without dietary preferences benefit from the signage, since it looks more professional and helps service run more smoothly, avoiding hassles and delays for all.

Tips

Clear signage can benefit more than just those with dietary preferences. While researching this book, I spoke with Victoria Williams, founder and CEO of terptree, an organization aimed at creating excellent experiences for deaf customers and employees. During our conversation, I realised that improved signage and visual communication aimed at dietary inclusivity would also better serve deaf or hard of hearing customers (one out of every six people in the UK), regardless of their dietary preferences. The deaf community is also made up of Common Denominators who need confidence in consistent service when they choose a place to eat. More from terptree is available at *bonuschapter.heatherlandex.com.*

A pre-order system

Do you want to establish your hotel as inclusive of those with dietary preferences? Imagine this sign at the reception:
"We invite you to let us know about any food allergies, intolerances or other dietary needs. Ask us for details about possibilities for an individual breakfast plate in place of our breakfast buffet. Please make requests the evening before."

Such an offer is particularly appropriate when the breakfast buffet is included in the price of the room. Some hotels already offer room service for early morning check-outs, but this is a new kind of customer service focused on inclusivity. If this service is introduced, make sure to put it on your website (alongside possible inclusions) and mention whether your staff are "allergy aware" to reach those who are looking for allergy-friendly options. But, as always, make sure you have the training and processes in place to deliver what you promise.

Each of these steps—mindset, alignment, plan, people, systems—takes you closer to true inclusivity. However, none of them can ensure progress if any one is missing.

Finally, a word of caution:
You cannot half-do inclusivity of a particular excluded group. There's a reason that mindset is the first step toward change. ***If you are not 100% in, you need to be out.*** You must commit 100% to safety. Do not steam ahead with menu changes without first going through the steps outlined in this chapter.

Maybe you aren't tempted to steam ahead. Perhaps, instead, you are worried about the risks of serving customers who require particular care. Fear of liability can be blinding. As a compliance consultant, I understand. I am well insured, and I also believe in continuous professional development and learning. I get it: it's a new thing to encourage people towards allergy friendliness. But ***not adapting to the market also carries risk.***

My advice? Commit to learning and investing in training, and you will grow more confident and competent on your journey toward inclusivity.

Guarantee safety, guarantee confidence.
You can always begin with initial research. Take stock of what skills and resources you currently have, **always starting with whether you need to improve your basic food safety standards first.** Once those are rock-solid, ask new questions. Are you not inclusive or are you quite inclusive? Have you suddenly realised you have more to offer than you first imagined?

No matter where you are on your inclusivity journey—or where you want to be—innumerable resources exist to help you on your way.

Takeaways

● The first step is Mindset (then Alignment, Plan, People, Systems).
● Build on food safety as a marketing strategy.
● Communication is extremely important.
● Staff need to know their role as part of a well-oiled machine.

Free Resources

You can find more examples at
bonuschapter.heatherlandex.com

There are free resources, links to helpful information, statistics and more at **freeresources.heatherlandex.com**

If you need help with delivering training or creating a bespoke training, or if you would like an inclusivity audit, contact me for an informal chat at **heather@heatherlandex.com**

Chapter 13

Fine Print, Legal Considerations, Fairness

Disclaimer: This is an opinions-based book and should not be interpreted as legal advice for your specific location, circumstances or business. Instead, I have done my best to provide simplified information of general interest.

In this chapter:
Legal considerations
Legislation changes
Legality does not equal morality
Fairness
Responsibility, risk and reward
On allergies and vegan claims
On certifications
The 1:10 rule

13.1 What are the laws covering dietary preferences?

The purpose of this book isn't to explore specific legislation or requirements (or what those mean in your situation), but I do want to touch on some examples from my part of the industry.

In the EU, there is a focus on **protecting the consumer's interests.** *"Food law shall aim at the protection of the interests of consumers and shall provide a basis for consumers to make informed choices in relation to the foods they consume."*

Regulation (EC) 178/2002 –General Food Law | Food Safety
According to the European Commission, legislation aims to prevent:
A) fraudulent or deceptive practices;
B) the adulteration of food; and
C) any other practices which may mislead the consumer.

In the UK, the **FSA** (Food Safety Act 1990) summary reads:
The main responsibilities for all food businesses under the Act are to ensure that:
  • *Businesses do not include anything in food, remove anything from food or treat food in any way which means it would be damaging to the health of people eating it;*
  • *The food businesses serve or sell is of the nature, substance or quality which consumers would expect;*
  • *The food is labelled, advertised and presented in a way that is not false or misleading.*

If you want to include people with dietary preferences to increase your customer base, you have to know what you are doing and not invite liability, litigation, scandal or complaints. Much of the risk associated with including more allergy sufferers, vegans or those with religiously motivated diets involves the possibility of ***contamination*** (i.e., stuff in food we don't want in the food) ***or insufficient or unclear disclosure.***

13.2 Legislation changes

Legislation changes over time. It adapts, becomes more complicated, addresses new concerns. If you take only one thing from this section, I hope it is this: businesses focus primarily on what they are ***legally required*** to do.
While that basic compliance is crucial, it's also often not enough.
  The stronger your food safety systems are now and the more you already do to manage allergies and reduce contamination, the better you can protect your customers, your brand and your ability to adapt to changing legislation.

129

Example:

From October 2021, the UK will implement **"Natasha's Law"**, requiring new allergy labelling requirements in the food service industry. Natasha's Law was driven in part by a media storm following high-profile allergy deaths (including a girl named Natasha), which increased public awareness and expectations around allergy management.

PRET A MANGER TO BRING IN FULL LABELLING AFTER TEENAGER'S DEATH

– 3 October 2018, The Guardian, UK

Pret a Manger reacted to Natasha's death by going beyond basic compliance. To protect their brand from any repeat high-profile cases, they brought in additional allergy labelling ahead of the legal requirement. The change is important—but if the company had gone beyond the minimum legal requirement earlier, Natasha's death might have been avoided altogether.

Legislation changes aren't just limited to food safety. They may also include laws regarding discrimination.

Inclusivity = the opposite of discrimination

In his book *Ethical Vegan,* **Jordi Casamitjana** describes his experiences during a high-profile employment tribunal in the UK. The tribunal found his employment was wrongfully terminated and gave Ethical Veganism, a philosophical belief, protection under the Equality Act 2010.

The change has set a precedent which other countries may follow. Legally, Ethical Veganism is now seen on similar footing to a religion. It's not yet clear how or if such a change will have compliance consequences for food manufacturing or food service, but it's a reason to start considering whether and how your business can treat vegan dietary preferences with the same strict quality and safety systems needed for halal and kosher requests.

Food service businesses can wait for the laws to change, but it doesn't always benefit them to do so. In my professional role (as a compliance specialist) and in my personal life (as a person dining out with dietary preferences), I can tell you that basic compliance is the bare minimum. Literally. It is exactly what is required to operate legally (i.e., not be subject to criminal charges). That's true for non-discrimination legislation, it's true for allergen safety legislation and it's true for training requirements. It's part of why legislation around food safety changes and evolves: we discover ways to do things more safely or more ethically.

13.3 Legality does not equal morality...
and the border between "legal" and "moral" isn't fixed.
One of the best things you can do for your business and your customers is to go beyond the bare legal minimum. That kind of change demands a change in mindset. By changing their mindset, business owners and staff will set—and reach—higher standards in food safety, inclusion and training. That protects both the business and the customer, and it makes all parties feel more confident.

There is currently a legal gap regarding both accessibility and contamination of food for these minority groups, whether that be in meeting the needs of those with halal or vegan diets, or those with food allergies or intolerances. As shown in the examples above, some of the people who are excluded or at-risk (from contamination) are working to change the laws. This movement goes beyond food law and into respect for human differences and diversity. It's a question of ethics.

131

Carissa Kranz, US—founding attorney and CEO of BeVeg International, global vegan certification firm

In our constitution, there's separation of church and state, and you can't be discriminated against for your religion. There's protection for religion and—to many of us— veganism is something we practice religiously.

If there's a separation of church and state, who is the government to tell us that our moral system and moral compass doesn't count as a religion when it's an entire movement based on a firmly held belief system?

There's a whole education and evolution of rights to protect here, and that's what to focus on.

The legislation in the area of veganism specifically is evolving, as seen in Jordi's tribunal. A look at related cases offers some insight into both the potential for bad press and the possible legal consequences of exclusion or poor attempts at inclusion.

Laura Chepner, UK— Primary Veducation, author of *An Educator's Guide for Vegan-Inclusive Teaching*

When my daughter started school, we were told that she was not eligible for free school meals based on the fact that she was vegan. Almost immediately, Primary Veducation Consultancy was born. We won this unprecedented fight and now every school in our borough can request a vegan menu.

VEGAN SUES BURGER KING FOR COOKING IMPOSSIBLE WHOPPER ON MEAT GRILL

—BBC, 20 November 2019
In this case, a vegan attempted to file a class action against

Burger King for cooking the Impossible Whopper alongside beef burgers, despite "100% Whopper, 0% meat" claims.

At the time of writing, there is no legislation regarding thresholds of contamination of animal products in plant-based options. The Impossible Whopper was not advertised as "suitable for vegans or vegetarians", and the case was rejected.

Because food services in schools, hospitals, childcare institutions and care homes operate under an obligation for duty of care, they have different responsibilities regarding inclusion than other areas of food service. Other businesses have no responsibility to include people. But it's ethical to do so, and it can gain businesses a very loyal following.

Who bears responsibility?

Jacqui McPeake, UK—owner of JACS Ltd. (food allergen and catering specialist) and former head of catering at a large university

Over the last 12 months, there has been a change in signage because of the...deaths we have heard about [in the media]. Negative signage. One I saw was, "We have trained our staff to the best of our ability; however, we cannot guarantee anything. In fact, if you are made poorly after you have eaten here, we will not be held liable."

And I'm thinking, "Oh my god, yes you will."

Stuart Ewen, UK—partner and co-founder of Mindset Associates

Where does the education piece start? Who takes responsibility? This is an interesting dynamic for me. Is it the consumer who needs to take responsibility, or is it the company? Or is it a shared joint responsibility that they both need to work to?

Legally, neither party automatically assumes responsibility when an adverse allergy event occurs. However, the business is liable if they misinform the consumer about the presence of any allergens they are required to disclose in their country. Therefore, I recommend as a courtesy and additional protection that the business train staff to ask all customers if there are any allergies, intolerances or dietary preferences as they seat them (in a restaurant scenario or similar).

Staff may expect customers to take the initiative of mentioning their allergy, but that doesn't always happen. Invite or teach your customers (with cues and gentle reminders) to inform you.

It is the business' responsibility to serve safe food, give accurate information and train their staff. *In my opinion,* it is the consumer's responsibility to inform the business about allergies and dietary preferences...but customers need to know that, and how to do it. Based on the business' response, the customer must then make a choice about risk. This choice can be challenging because of complications in food labelling, contamination concerns and ingredient components that are not easily identified as a risk. The level of risk is not quantified. The more information you can provide, the easier the customer's decision will be.

Public awareness is a difficult thing to master.
One thing you can control is your staff's level of awareness and training.

13.4 Fairness

Fairness is also part of inclusivity considerations, and I don't only mean for the customer. Having inclusivity as a core part of mindset—with established systems for tracking and communicating allergens, as well as at least one widely inclusive dish on the menu—creates a better, fairer work environment for staff preparing food. It is **unfair** to put responsibility on the chef to create a bespoke option for the customer without prior thought to the kitchen layout, time and mental energy needed, availability of ingredients and information about the ingredients...all while using a server's second-hand description of the customer's dietary preference. Chefs often have the competency and creativity to serve people with dietary preferences something amazing, but their hands are tied because they lack resources and systems.

On training and awareness

I have done some pro bono work in Copenhagen with a not-for-profit restaurant called OneBowl. The community-centred restaurant is a plant-based concept, and its name was chosen to reflect that it is a place where all are welcome, regardless of their ability to pay.

My conversations and experiences at OneBowl highlighted some of the inequalities small community businesses face when it comes to inclusivity, safety and liability. A food business may open without any help in understanding food compliance and what is required for safety. Small businesses may not have a budget for tech, compliance consultants or outsourced training. Many not-for-profits, charities and community groups rely on well-intentioned volunteers, who may have limited experience or knowledge.

The food inspectors may come and give official advice or instructions, but there are very few free resources for training. In the UK, the FSA has published some booklets ("Safer Food, Better Business"), and here in Denmark, Foedvarestyrelsen (the Danish Veterinary and Food Administration) provides some standard risk assessment templates, but small businesses and the general public are vulnerable to mistakes through no fault of their own. Food hygiene, allergy awareness and inclusivity are not courses taught in most schools and mastering them in a commercial kitchen requires a lot more than "common sense".

> **Caron Pollard, UK—allergy mum and digital marketing expert, co-founder of Teal App**
> *There is such a lack of knowledge and awareness from people that are not exposed to allergies. We see it in so many aspects of our lives, which turns us into helicopter mums and dads, filled with anxiety. Year-on-year hospital admissions for allergic reactions are increasing, most allergic incidents occur outside the home and reactions peak at adolescence. All these facts support the argument for better awareness and education around allergies.*

Perhaps it should be compulsory to learn about food safety or allergy awareness in schools as a critical life skill. Or, for the sake of public safety and inclusion, there could be a compulsory course or certification when a food business is first registered. Today's online technology would help make it more cost-effective in the long run, especially considering the rise in food allergies, intolerances or related issues and the number of people getting sick from food.

Millions of people are affected by food poisoning.
Millions of people are affected by allergies and intolerances.
Just in the UK alone.

Learning more about food safety from an inclusion perspective will allow you to safely serve a wide variety of customers: those with allergies and intolerances, those with health conditions, those with religiously or ethically motivated diets—and anyone else who walks through your doors.

13.5 Risks and rewards

There are no limits to the fines for food safety offences in the UK. The bigger the company, the bigger the risk.

However, you cannot sit back and do **NOTHING** in regard to allergy management. A vegan restaurant owner once told me she didn't want to "take on that kind of responsibility" in regard to serving allergy sufferers. But you cannot escape it—those with allergies are everywhere (including in a vegan restaurant). All these groups are a part of society, and I can pretty much guarantee that some of them are dining with you already. You are already required to provide allergen information; why not present it in such a way that people can more easily make informed choices and trust your competency?

Sending allergy sufferers away (although they may be used to it) damages your reputation. Serving them poorly or unsafely may harm them. You will certainly lose their business, and you also risk bad press and litigation. You may also be out-competed by the businesses who *are* working to include these growing markets. These days, people care about the values of the companies they support, and key issues tied to "atypical" diets (e.g., diversity, inclusiveness,

health and environmentalism) have become increasingly mainstream and important. Businesses that don't adapt are vulnerable
to looking outdated and being left behind.

13.6 Claims and labelling

The basic labelling requirement is to provide accurate allergy
information about the food. In the UK, that information has to
be communicated between all the links of the supply chain. The
intention of labelling laws is to inform consumers in order to
protect them from injury, death or suffering. However, labelling
standards leave room for improvement. For example, basic compliance only requires that the allergen information be provided
and that allergens are listed *and emphasised* on packaged food—
individual manufacturers may use different forms of emphasis.

> **Caron Pollard, UK—allergy mum and digital marketing
> expert, co-founder of Teal App**
> *Some of the challenges of food allergies include inconsistent la-
> belling on food and beverage products. This leads to confusion
> as there is no standardised rule to adhere to and important
> information around food safety — like allergens listed—can
> be missed. What would be more helpful is to have one form of
> allergens labelling; that is, to emphasise allergens in bold.*
>
> *In 2020 alone there have been over 70 allergy-related
> product recalls in the UK, with over 80% a result of undeclared
> allergens or incorrect labelling [NB: data was current as of our
> interview in late 2020]. There is no current recourse for action.
> Instead, the public is to return or discard the products. This is
> a risky strategy, which may result in the ultimate price being
> paid as a result of this negligent error.*
>
> *The lack of standardised grading and labelling also means that
> "may contain" disclaimers are open to interpretation. When the
> consumer relies on that information to make an informed deci-
> sion around allergy safety, it does not inspire confidence. As a re-
> sult, many people steer clear of "may contain"-labelled products,
> which in some cases could be costing the business unnecessarily.*

The issues and inconsistencies with labelling also have consequences in food service. In the UK, for example, food service businesses often take on extra responsibility because many manufacturers use "may contain" disclaimers or provide allergy information in a way which cannot easily be understood or used by the caterer or chef. However, it is only the food manufacturer's responsibility to provide allergy information and honour food safety requirements. They are not obligated to make it easy for the rest of the supply chain, particularly if there is no explicit demand for it.

> **Tarryn Gorre, UK—CEO and co-founder at Kafoodle, a fast-growing food-tech company matching people to food within the education, hospitality and healthcare spaces**
> *The difficulty food businesses have, from my experience, is that food manufacturers are not always being held accountable enough. When they [food service businesses] buy products, the manufacturer might have disclaimers saying "may contain", but it is the restaurant getting the backlash from the consumer.*

With many food manufacturers, there seems to be no compromise: labels are printed with either "free from" or "may contain". In a setting where foods are served without packaging (e.g., a restaurant or café), I would suggest you direct people to the information and make it as comprehensive as possible. For example, was it vegan/gluten-free/peanut-free and without disclaimers when it came in? Is that still true when it is served to the customer, or is it likely contaminated? If it is likely to be contaminated, state it. If it is very unlikely to be contaminated, please state that too rather than defaulting to a nonspecific, automatic "may contain" or "traces of" disclaimer (see Chapter 14 for appropriate wording on menus).

David McGee, UK—director at Hayfields Consultancy Ltd., the UK's only vegan consultant (Free From, BRCGS[7], Retailers SME)

There are methods of handling allergens at manufacturer factory sites in order to prevent contamination and avoid alibi labelling. Manufacturers may not go to any great effort to avoid "may contain" on vegan products. Perhaps they think alibi labelling is the safest, most responsible thing to do because they have an allergen in the factory.

Alibi labelling can be seen as the convenient way of attempting to meet labelling regulations, but it is not fair to consumers.

There are more details about manufacturers from David at **bonuschapter.heatherlandex.com**.

Yes, the risk from not being honest and transparent about possible "traces of" is high, since you have to factor in that you may offend passionate activists if contamination is present. I am not only referring to vegans and environmentalists, but also to those campaigning for better conditions for those with allergies or intolerances, or those working to expand options for people who share their religion. I understand why companies want to default to such disclaimers. However, whenever possible, it is in the customer's interests to learn and disclose as much as possible about the actual risk level rather than using alibi labelling as a shield. By doing so, you offer the customer both choice and peace of mind.

13.7 How are certifications, approvals and label claims regulated?

The short answer is that it depends on the certification, approval or label. Here, however, I'm mostly going to focus on the regulations for allergen labelling and vegan claims, since misunder-

---

7   *BRCGS, or Brand Reputation through Compliance Global Standards (formerly British Retail Consortium), is a global food safety standard and certification organization.*

standing the limitations of each can have serious consequences.

First and foremost, **vegan labels on manufactured products are not necessarily regulated**. Vegans are sometimes upset to find that products that appear to be vegan in mainstream restaurants are not. In other cases, however, the issue occurs not in the restaurant, but where food is manufactured.

> **Mette Johannsen—office manager at Dansk Vegetarisk Forening, "Det Grønne Hjerte" og "V-Label" (The Vegetarian Society of Denmark, The Green Heart and V-Label)**
> *I think right now we have to find some sort of pragmatic level where we say this is as far as we can go because otherwise, we couldn't label anything. We tolerate "may contain" because we do accept products that are produced in the same factory, sometimes on the same line. We have guidelines for cleaning, we look into all the ingredients but we do not test the ingredients.*

Since there is no legal guidance as to what may be classed as vegan or cruelty-free, different organizations offer their own guidance and certification. The Vegan Society UK offer both a definition of vegan and their own stamp of approval, which is based in thorough research of the ingredients and the word of the manufacturer. **V-label** does as well. There is also a new **BeVeg** certification, which offers more guarantees than traditional vegan trademarks, and which will soon expand to include a restaurant standard.

> **Carissa Kranz, US—founding attorney and CEO of BeVeg International, global vegan certification firm**
> *There are other vegan trademarks...but anyone can get a global trademark. All you need to do is write a logo on a napkin and pay your trademark fee. That is very different than an accredited global vegan standard like BeVeg, which is technical and systematic in approach, with gap analysis, root analysis, cross-contamination analysis and onsite audits, lab testing for animal DNA, and more.*

> *BeVeg is audited by accreditation centers and held account-able. That is very different from other well-intentioned vegan trademarks.*

The eligibility criteria for certifications are discussed at **bonus-chapter.heatherlandex.com.**

Because the labelling for vegan products has been largely unregulated, **problems can occur when customers with, for example, milk or egg allergies assume packaged products with a vegan logo stamped on the front are "safe"**, or that a vegan dish in a restaurant will be free from fish contamination. *As of the writing of this book, vegan-labelled products are not guaranteed to be free from milk or egg.* It is unsurprising, then that the recommendation from the UK Food and Drink Federation (February 2020) reads as follows:
"Consumers should not rely on a 'vegan' logo if they have milk, fish, crustacean, mollusc and/or egg food allergies."

If it doesn't say 'Allergen'-Free, do not assume it is! Manufacturers' labels must not say or suggest 'Allergen'-Free unless the food is assured to be absent of the specified allergen. "Free-from" claims are absolutes (guaranteed 0.000% chance of contamination) and often require verification. If the manufac-turer were to be misleading and cause injury to consumers with intolerances or allergies, the manufacturer would be held liable for food safety offences. For that reason, many vegan labels carry the "may contain" and "traces of" disclaimers; their products are ***not*** marketed for the allergy sufferer. There is also another mech-anism at work with alibi labelling: if the manufacturer doesn't use a disclaimer, they are more liable to have to recall should undisclosed allergens (allergens not mentioned on the label) be present—a very expensive process.

David McGee, UK—director at Hayfields Consultancy Ltd., the UK's only vegan consultant (Free From, BRCGS, Retailers SME)
"If a manufacturer makes a vegan claim, the consumer reading that label will not read the legal bit—the alibi labelling—because there is this big vegan symbol on the packet.

There are obvious food safety issues. FSA often has recalls due to allergens with vegan trademarks on labels. It will only take one food scare to cause an issue.

Most manufacturers, even with BRC [Brand Reputation Compliance] certification, may not realise that they need to document their justification for alibi labelling as part of their HACCP [Hazard Analysis Critical Control Point] systems.

They have to prove that they cannot avoid it, which is the bit they get confused about.

When possible, avoid disclaimers on your ingredients. Choose free-from labels when available (although they usually come at a premium), absent of "may contain" alibis, or make everything yourself from the raw ingredients so that you can be in charge of your own claims. Fresh, minimally processed foods with a small carbon footprint also have a growing market, which is another bonus of making the foods yourself.

When you must use packaged ingredients and the supplier or manufacturer has a "may contain" label, request risk assessment information. A "made on the same line as X, Y and Z" warning is very different to a "made in the same factory as X, Y or Z" warning, and your customer is likely to appreciate the distinction.

Risk assessment information is useful for other claims as well, such as vegan. When claims like "suitable for vegans", "suitable for vegetarians" or "not suitable for or vegetarians" are used, no explanation is legally required. However, I would find that information extremely useful. *Is it vegan or not? If not, why not?* Often packaging will state that the product is suitable for vegetarians when in fact it is also suitable for vegans. Again, ask questions of the supplier or manufacturer so you can share clear information with your customer.

Make sure to consider the way your product is prepared as well, and how that may be made more inclusive. The Burger King lawsuit earlier in this chapter is a good example of a product that a consumer assumed to be vegan but was in actuality plant-based...and it was cooked on the same grill as meat and served by default with mayonnaise (containing egg). Similar critiques can be made of McDonald's new McPlant, which is topped with cheddar cheese and mayo and cooked on a shared grill. Big, high-volume businesses tend to aim for the flexitarians and meat-reducers, which means that smaller businesses have a chance to shine in ways that will attract the people who need a more specialised approach (the other end of the plant-based continuum).

Note
Absence of *"may contain"* doesn't equal *"free from"*

First, "may contain" disclaimers are voluntary, not required.

Second, allergy risk information in, for example, restaurants, is a record of the ingredients and may not reflect the restaurant's allergy management practices.

And finally, there is always the risk of human error (and misunderstanding) at any step in the food chain.

Things change...

Because of the problems created by the lack of legal standards for vegetarian and vegan claims, the up-and-coming BeVeg certification is a significantly different certification to what has come before. Food manufacturers have to meet a vigorous set of standards for ensuring zero contamination—that is, *a clean vegan stamp,* which would also be a useful tool for those with milk and egg allergies. The BeVeg certification was founded by Carissa

Kranz, a lawyer and life-long vegan from the US. This 100% vegan trademark is intended for all aspects of life, from fashion to cosmetics to businesses.

I was the expert advisor consulted in the development of the restaurant/services portion of the BeVeg standard, which is the first and only ISO accredited vegan certification standard in the world. I currently serve on the BeVeg executive team as Chief Compliance Officer for the restaurant/hospitality sector and head up the related BeVeg vegan training program.

13.8 The 1:10 Rule

There is no such thing as zero risk. Every once in a while, despite food safety management systems, trainings and compliance checks, things may go wrong. Someone will complain. And when they do, the way your business responds matters.

Always take complaints as an opportunity to learn and correct, even if you feel like your customers are generally happy. Why?

The 1:10 rule
If one person complains, there are at least 9 others that didn't say anything

This general guideline applies to complaints about customer service, food poisoning, allergy incidents—pretty much anything you can imagine. Many people don't formally complain because they don't want to seem difficult, it's too much effort or they do not know how to report an issue. For that reason, the people who do report are a great opportunity to take action to prevent future incidents, especially any *serious* incidents. I recommend you have a clear complaints procedure, so you can capture that one person's perspective and address it properly.

"But we've never had an incident or complaint, yet."
This attitude—whether it's used to explain away bare-minimum contamination management or to justify why there is no standard

complaints procedure—makes me want to ***scream*** as an Environmental Health Practitioner. Driving without a seatbelt doesn't mean you will have an accident. And even if you do have an accident, it doesn't mean you'll *die* in that accident. However, you must consider ***how much risk you are willing to take.***

Don't ever give your customers a reason to doubt you.

Besides, if you don't have a system in place to gather and respond to complaints, you can't fairly evaluate whether you are getting them.

Example:

Once, when I was travelling and had to eat at an airport, the food I ordered smelt of disinfectant or chlorine. The server admitted they had just cleaned the dishwasher but did not offer to replace my meal. Instead, she laughed it off.

I reported them to Environmental Health at the local council.

Not only were they serving unfit food, but the response to my complaint was also "concerning" (by which I meant "***infuriating***" and "***potentially dangerous***".) Complaints should always be taken seriously and handled swiftly.

Surviving uninjured after eating a meal is not a good enough standard of safety protection for me, or the law. It does not prove the risk was low just because something ***didn't*** happen or because nobody complained about it ***on record***.

Always remember the 1:10 rule.

At the airport, the server probably never mentioned my complaint to a supervisor or manager. I would have liked to have seen her write it down. I'd also have liked someone to do something to correct the problem with the dishwasher and report back to me, immediately. They should also have replaced my meal with a non-contaminated one.

Legal minimum requirements are not enough to ensure brand protection. Consider the risks, the opportunities, and your capabilities, then make a plan and consistently stick to it.

145

Generally, you may take or leave my suggestions in this book, but ***please DO take onboard safety warnings***. Do your own research and build your own wisdom in this matter; it will serve you well in the future. I have included a bibliography and links to free resources to help you further educate yourself, specific to your needs.

Free Resources

Free resources such as links, campaigns and statistics can be found at **freeresources.heatherlandex.com**

Bonus chapters with contributions for David and Caron, plus discussion of Natasha's Law in the UK, can be found at
bonuschapter.heatherlandex.com
Also included: a list of vegan certifications criteria.

If you need help or advice with wording, allergy management, communication and marketing or other steps on the way to improving inclusivity, please do get in touch at
heather@heatherlandex.com

Chapter 14

Inclusivity Marketing Tips

In this chapter:
Keywords and SEO
Online menus
Substitutions and price
Signs, cues, little *notices
Feedback
The "must-do's"

I've said it before, but it's worth repeating: I'm not asking you to change your core concept. I'm encouraging you to think about how you can expand what you offer to reach more customers and avoid leaving money on the table. Niche marketing opportunities exist for food service businesses that are able to cater to dietary preferences. In this chapter, I've collected expert input that will help you think about how to market your inclusivity efforts and boost their success.

14.1 Getting the word out: Keywords and SEO

Hartej Kahai, Canada—Your Vegan Marketer, a digital marketer, customer acquisition, paid search and off-page SEO consultant

From an SEO [Search Engine Optimization] point of view for restaurants, have a page that screams and shouts what you're doing, because what you're doing is amazing. It's incredible. But we need to tell Google that. Google needs to see that from a robot perspective, and robots only pick up words and content in articles or posts. An allergen list, pdf file or even a filterable menu—Google's not going to pick up on it.

> *What a restaurant can do is to have **a dedicated page—a content page or blog**—on their website explaining exactly what they're doing to cater to different dietary needs. **A dedicated page** that talks about how they are friendly for vegans, or how they are catering for gluten intolerance, how they are catering for allergies. Then eventually Google will start to pick up on that.*
>
> *For example, if someone searches for "vegan options restaurant" or "vegan restaurant" in Dubai, Google displays a map and three restaurants. Always. And then if you click "more", you see the whole list [of restaurants]. So, what we do for our clients is help them get their site to be one of the top three. And the benefit of that is that not only people in Dubai searching for restaurants will see it, but also people planning travel to Dubai—anyone who searches will see those as the top three. They're likely to put one of those three in their itinerary, and then that restaurant will get the business.*

It's hard work to do inclusivity well, so show off when you do! On social media, websites, delivery apps and adverts, include keywords relevant for the inclusive options you consistently have available, like *vegan, vegetarian, gluten-free, allergy-friendly.* Share photos of your food. If you are top-listed on Google, customers will enjoy seeing photos and reviews from other customers.

14.2 Improve your online menus

Interactive menus/websites/QR codes have been mentioned and recommended throughout the book. These tools are a sensible investment in the post-pandemic world generally, but they also appeal to the increasing number of those with allergies, intolerances and/or plant-based diets.

Case Study 1: (Disclaimer: I do not currently, nor have I ever, worked with or in association with The Lounges.)

In October 2020, The Lounges (thelounges.co.uk) had a very nice filter on their website menu. There was a vegan menu and a gluten-free menu, and you could also filter the menu for each of the EU's 14 allergens (e.g., milk, soya). It was an easy-to-use, attractive online menu, and it was very inclusive for several dietary preferences. I liked it.

However...

If the customer (me, in this case) wanted to exclude milk and did not accept **"may contain"** as an opt-in button at the top of the Dietary Preferences menu, the only options were a salad (non-vegan) or 3 vegan cakes. *If ever there was an excuse to eat cake for dinner!*

Remember, 23% of people in the UK avoid milk, according to Statista. It is a valuable USP when you can offer milk-free options on your menu. If I'd been a consultant for this restaurant, I would have recommended including a milk-free item on this menu or a MFO (Milk-Free Option) symbol, specifying that a dish can be made without milk on request. Additionally, the "may contain" button could trigger a notice to please contact the restaurant to ask about allergies, intolerances and dietary preferences so the customer can get a more detailed explanation.

As a user, I had questions that were not answered by the website. Could allergy sufferers talk to the restaurant directly? Could menu items be made "free-from"? Were the "may contain" disclaimers from manufacturers, or were they there because everything is cooked in/on/next to or using the same equipment/oil/grill as milk or cheese? Should I interpret the disclaimers as a fear of incidents, a lack of trust in the staff's skills and knowledge in the kitchen, or a lack of safe systems? Or was this just an oversight or tech issue?

I had all respect for The Lounges for having done as much as they had. It was great to see an efficient way for customers to make informed choices. But adding a notice could have encouraged someone with allergies or other contamination concerns to make a reservation, pre-order or comfortably notify staff, all of which would have increased the chances of them confidently choosing that restaurant.

By January 2021, The Lounges' menu had evolved. There was now a range of options available within the vegan menu, even when filtering for milk and disabling the "may contain" opt-in button.

Excitedly, I contacted them to ask what had motivated these changes.

I spoke with Jono Jenkins, Head of Food, who said:
"The criticism shows the challenges that even the best can find difficult.

For example, we don't declare that any fried items on our menu are vegan unless they have been cooked in the vegan fryer. We have one fryer that is gluten-free and vegan. It probably does limit our options when we develop new vegan dishes, because **we play to the strictest approach to veganism and the most severe allergy sufferers.** *Doing so allows us to segregate the allergens within our fryers and be very rigid and robust on that.*

Our teams are extremely good at providing information to our customers to inform and reassure them, almost opening the kitchen doors and letting them in to have a look. We have very specific cooking processes, certainly from an allergen per-spective. We have an extremely robust system in place, from the point of ordering to the point of delivery.

I think the manufacturers have been surprised by some of our requests and the detail that we've gone into. We put a huge amount of time and effort into taking it seriously.

I think the motivation, in terms of being responsible for building the food offer, is making sure that we're safe, but also making our customers happy and feel included.

The way we advertise best is by being inclusive in our sites. *It is our vegan, gluten-free and core menus which I think im-mediately give our customers the reassurance that they can come to our sites and get a broader experience as a guest. It gives our customers reassurance that we're genuinely thinking about their dietary preferences and requirements. That leads to a perception and confidence that we also take allergies seriously. Obviously, our vegan and gluten-free menus don't cover all 14 [EU] allergens, so for this we provide a very clear allergen matrix by dish. But I think the individual menus are a very good starting point.*

We really care about everybody walking into our Lounge. I think that is an unbelievably important approach."

150

While chatting with Jono, I recommended HappyCow, Teal App and marketing through local vegans to their area's social media groups. I also recommended SEO improvements following Hartej's advice at the beginning of this chapter, as well as the suggestion to include a notice with the "may contain" button to prompt customers to inform the business of their dietary preferences and ask about possible options when ordering. When I find a business working as hard toward inclusivity as The Lounges does, I want everyone to know about them!

14.3 Be thoughtful about substitutions and pricing

When you offer menu options that can be customized according to dietary preferences, make sure the pricing structure feels fair to the customer.

Example 1:

There is a more luxurious build-a-burger chain in Denmark. Customers choose from among several patty options (including three different vegetarian patties) and several recommended, named topping combinations for the burgers. The chain is child-friendly and all-around brilliant, and I've had wonderful service there.

However...

When you order takeaway online, the experience of customizing a vegan burger is different. When dining in, there's a modest upcharge for substituting vegan toppings, but when using takeaway, the vegan cheese and vegan sauces ***stack up as extras rather than substitutions***. As a result, the total price for my takeaway vegan burger would have been a full 50% more than the equivalent takeaway non-vegan burger.

Like me, many customers are likely to be confused or frustrated if the pricing for their inclusive option includes *both* the cost of each of the "typical" toppings *and* the full price of the inclusive substitutions as add-ons. It is likely an oversight, and I have written to them to let them know that the current online delivery menu is not especially inclusive.

> **Tip**
>
> As a business, make the **ordering and buying decision as easy and as fair as possible. Customers will notice.**

Example 2:
I love **Zócalo,** a Swedish company at Tivoli Street Food in Copenhagen with great signage that invites customization.

"Vegan or vegetarian? Every single item on the menu can be vegan or vegetarian, just pick a vegan protein option and we'll fix the rest."

Anything can be made vegan by substitution at no extra cost. I also like that I can watch them make it.

> **Tip**
>
> When setting your prices, keep in mind your customer perception of value. Look for ways to develop tasty, interesting dishes that are not disproportionately costly.

Make the exception and be exceptional. Treat people with dietary preferences equally as well as typical eaters.

14.4 How to use signs, cues or little *notices

Written notices and visual cues can help a great deal in subtly communicating your inclusivity efforts, but it can be challenging to figure out the most user-friendly way of presenting the information.

Case Study 2: Apres Food Co., UK
I recently contacted Apres Food Co. to inquire about nuts on their online menu, as I thought I'd found a discrepancy between the menu and the extensive allergen information. The response I received was quite impressive.

Catherine Sharman, UK—Apres Food Co.

"I'm not sure how else we could make this [allergen informa-tion] clearer on the menu without it overwhelming the descrip-tion of the food and enjoyment of reading it.

Part of the dilemma is there are so many options, as I make everything from scratch. For example, dairy dishes may be available without dairy, so every dish would need a separate sentence about the different options available.

It's far friendlier (and preferable) for us to actually chat to our customers and customise their meal however they would like it. I think part of the problem in the hospitality sector is that there are barriers between customers and chefs, with chefs being unwilling or unable to customise things. So, we not only make nearly every dish customisable but also chat with our customers before they order. "

I completely agreed with her response, and I suggested that she consider adding the last paragraph to the bottom of the menu. It reflects exceptional service that not every place can offer.

Tip

A welcoming message like this on a menu builds trust and encourages communication. By allowing for things to be customized (e.g., as gluten-free or vegan) to fit different dietary preferences, it also advertises a unique selling point and gives an impression of quality. All without overcrowd-ing the menu with icons or explanations.

I wasn't surprised to see the list of awards on Apres Food Co.'s website. They have been distinguished as *Time Out's* Best Healthy Restaurant in London (January 2020), Forbes' Best Gluten Free Restaurant in London and *Tatler's* Best Breakfast in London. They have also won gold in the 2019 Free From Awards.

Understand your USPs.

Apres Food Co.'s approach is smart business. Always encourage customers to tell you about allergies or other dietary preferences. It can be especially helpful to invite them to give advance notice of their needs or pre-order 24–48 hours ahead of arrival. Doing so allows chefs to plan a special dish if needed, and kitchen staff can separate ingredients before they are put into a makeline.

Not all customers will think to or be able to give advance notice, however, so make sure you provide opportunities for them to tell you what you need to know about allergies, intolerances or other dietary preferences *before they order*. Make it easy. On booking and/or arrival, ask them if there are any allergies or intolerances. Post signage inviting people to ask about menu adaptations. Additionally, the appropriate staff can wear an *Ask me about allergies* badge, but it may be difficult to ask potentially complicated questions of a busy server. A *self-serve option* like a QR code, allergy matrix or specialized menu is best, but staff should show customers how to use it and be prepared to answer questions.

Tip

Moving specialized menus to QR codes can allow you to quickly and cheaply update information as needed. For customers without smart phones, however, it's good to keep a print copy on hand, or ensure the business can print one on demand.

More to consider when communicating inclusive options

• Ideally, **indicators of inclusiveness** are clear to those who need them without being off-putting to those who don't need them. "Typical" eaters are unlikely to choose foods from a special vegan or gluten-free section on the menu, but they may choose a slice of cake that has a subtle GF (gluten free) in the margin next to it.

> **Chris Jenner, UK—insight manager at Winterbotham Darby & Co., with a background in Maths and Applied Statistics, and a BA in Economics from the University of Cambridge**
> *The flexitarian is king in the meat-free space, making up the majority of shoppers and spend. In the interest of the overall category performance, therefore, I would be nervous about making changes that could potentially alienate them. If, however, a helpful messaging change can be made for the dietary-restricted shoppers without impacting the flexitarians, then that's clearly positive.*

● **Choose indicators that are easily understood.** Picture- or shape-based allergen icons are not standardised and can be easy to misinterpret. For example, the bean-shaped icon for soya may be hard to tell apart from a similar icon for eggs. If you do choose shape-based allergen icons, consider including less-ambiguous letters on the images. (E.g., GF for gluten-free, GFO for gluten-free option available, VG for vegan, VGO for vegan option available, V for vegetarian, MFO for milk-free option available, H for halal, etc.) Consider using asterisks* and footnotes to indicate that an item can be made without [ingredient/allergen]. **Make sure a key is present and that the customer knows where to find it!**

● **List any relevant certifications** (e.g., halal) on the bottom of the menu where you have your icon key, or on the back of the menu where you may have your simplified allergen information and QR codes. These are also good spots for the anti-disclaimer disclaimer: If you have separation of certain foods or are naturally free of a certain allergen in your kitchen, state it. E.g., *Peanut-free kitchen* or **All gluten-free foods prepared separately on dedicated gluten-free equipment.*

● **Do prompt customers to ask about the specific item they want to order.** Long or complex menus might distract or confuse them. Simplified allergy information may indicate food is appropriate without information about "traces of" or "may contain".

❥ As a safety measure and to increase customer confidence, staff in applicable contexts should also be trained to **repeat a customer's order back to them** to confirm the information is correct, then repeat it **again when serving** them their food. **Guarantee safety, guarantee confidence.**

These tips save time. When staff can point customers toward the information in print or online, customers won't need to assume, wonder or ask lots of questions. Access to clear, understandable information reduces the customer's effort and makes it easier to upsell. Just remember to remind/prompt/encourage them to tell you about dietary preferences before ordering to ensure all necessary procedures are in place.

14.5 Seek out and learn from feedback

Ask questions. Conduct surveys. Encourage reviews. Seek out feedback from your customer base.

When you ask questions, make sure customers can give the feedback anonymously (via in-store feedback boxes, online surveys, etc.) and make sure that online surveys allow them to skip questions they may not want to answer.

Some things to investigate: Where did you first hear about us? Have you tried our new vegan option? Why or why not? Did you like it? Any suggestions? Were you able to find something to eat on our menu? Do you have any dietary preferences?

Remember the 1:10 rule. For every one complaint, there were nine others that didn't say anything. Perhaps the same is true for positive reviews. Regardless, you will benefit by encouraging feedback and making it easy and quick.

Get reviewed

❥ Tip 1: **Offer samples of your inclusive options or a voucher for a freebie in exchange for a review.** The tasters/reviewers do not need to have dietary preferences to promote your inclusive menu and improve your visibility in those niches, but it helps. If you have a customer or staff member who is (for example) vegan or eats a gluten-free diet, ask them whether they would be willing to sample the menu (with or without some friends) and review it in relevant local groups to which they belong.

🍷 Tip 2: **Reviews on HappyCow and Teal App can be especially helpful.** Put their logos on your website to encourage the Network Effect (links at **freeresources.heatherlandex.com**).

🍷 Tip 3: **Give out coupons (10% off next visit) in thanks for online surveys completed** and ask for permission to use survey comments in advertising.

🍷 Tip 4: **Offer a limited-time-only discount code for an inclusive option** you want to highlight. Promote it on social media and encourage sharing.

🍷 Tip 5: **Sponsor a related cause.** In the UK, for example, you might be a corporate sponsor of Anaphylaxis UK, seek GF Accreditation from Coeliac UK or publicly donate to the Natasha Allergy Research Foundation.

14.6 What are the "must do's"?

Remember the upsells: add-ons, sides, toppings, desserts, drinks! Everyone forgets the drinks, but both gluten-free and vegan customers will appreciate knowing which beers or wine are appropriate for them. (Fun fact: Guinness has been vegan since 2018!) Those who don't consume alcohol will also appreciate thoughtful celebratory drinks and non-alcoholic cocktails appropriate for them.

Extend extra kindness to parents of children with dietary needs. Children may also be vegan and/or have higher chance of allergies, while also being pickier-than-average eaters. Parents often have to bear the weight of ensuring their child's safety while distracted with other parenting tasks. I recommend compassion, patience and a bit of extra friendliness; it goes a long way toward making a potentially stressful situation better for everyone.

> **Caron Pollard, UK—allergy mum and digital marketing expert, co-founder of Teal App**
> *Eating out for us has been a mixed experience. For the most part, we have found that a limited number of establishments are able to cater for our daughter's allergies. We generally stick to them, as it provides peace of mind and a better dining experience for us....*
>
> *It really does not take much to satisfy an allergic customer. The secret formula: keep the lines of communication strong. Between the customer and the establishment, and between the front of the house, the management and the kitchen. And find an alternative solution when the menu can't cater. This has provided the best experiences for us and turned us into loyal advocates [of the businesses that do this], as they really understand the importance of the customer experience.*

Always be honest. If you cannot serve someone, do not exaggerate your capabilities. If you *can* serve them, don't turn them away just because it's inconvenient. Train your staff to be that way, too. ***Represent what you offer without greenwashing*** (making things seem more sustainable, healthy, vegan, etc. than they actually are). Marketers tend to want to stretch the wording, but this can backfire badly in the case of dietary preferences.

Realise there may be consequences to changing inclusive recipes or menus for some people. Having food allergies or intolerances often makes dining out of the home stressful, and many people rely on consistency and familiarity for safety. They want what they know and trust. And don't be too quick to pull an inclusive option that is selling below expectations. The sales volume of your inclusive options may not reflect the people coming along with the Common Denominator.

Prioritise keeping information up to date. Have procedures in place when menus, ingredients or suppliers change so that you can update allergen information promptly and easily.

Respect personal boundaries. Allergy sufferers or those with intolerances may not want to discuss all the details of their personal health or diet with you. Answer more questions than you ask, stick to the need-to-know topics, make sure you are clear on the ingredients they want to avoid and be able to describe how food is prepared and cooked (or know how and where to find out quickly).

Treat questions as questions, not as criticism. Don't take questions or reminders personally. A chef or server might feel frustrated that the customer doesn't seem to trust them, but it's not reasonable for a customer to trust their health (or life) to a stranger, particularly if they have had bad experiences in the past. Deliver great service, and they will trust you next time.

Be consistent and committed when it comes to inclusivity. You cannot consider people one day and ignore them the next. It's not good business to only offer a vegan dish for Veganuary (Vegan January) and then discontinue it. Likewise, keep inclusive options in stock. When you turn people away, that ripples out indefinitely via the Common Denominator and Network Effects.

Break away from the status quo. If there are no other vegan or allergy-friendly local restaurants, it's an opportunity, not an indication of lack of demand. ***Be first!***

Make brilliant food. Just because an inclusive option meets the technical definition of vegan or gluten-free or another dietary preference, that doesn't mean your customers will like it. Creativity, quality, flavour, presentation and perceived value matter just as much as they do for any other dish.

Takeaways

- Guarantee safety, guarantee confidence.
- Then shout about it!
- Inclusive Is the New Exclusive.

Free Resources

Bonus content at **bonuschapter.heatherlandex.com**

Free resources include links to statistics, campaigns, HappyCow stickers, free education and information.

freeresources.heatherlandex.com

You can download your own Teal App PDF colour poster at **teal.heatherlandex.com**

See also **Author Resources** at the back of the book.
If you want me to check your customer journey and optimise your marketing and communication, get in touch.

Heather@heatherlandex.com

Chapter 15

Inspiration for the Inclusive Menu

In this chapter:
Quick guide to inclusive options
Insights from the industry

It is my hope that this final chapter inspires you to create. The overarching point of this book is to help you offer appealing food that can serve as many people as possible. To help you on your way to being more inclusive (no matter your starting point!), I have summarised key advice and gathered some parting expert opinions.

15.1 Quick guide to inclusive options

A clean vegan option (free from animal contamination) can serve many dietary preferences including:
🍃 Those with allergies and intolerances to animal products, such as the 23% of people who avoid milk (Statista, UK)
🍃 Everyone on the plant-based continuum, including the meat-eaters who want to try something new
🍃 Some of those following religious diets that restrict specific animal products or require them to be prepared a certain way

When you please a vegan, you can please a lot of other people too.

To make the most of your inclusive menu:
- **Use a clean vegan base**
- **Reduce the number of ingredients** - leave out unnecessary allergens
- **Consider nutrition** - create a satiating, balanced meal with a good source of protein (and don't limit yourself to processed fake meat substitutes!)
- **Incorporate variety** - on the menu and within the dish...and don't add the same thing in each dish (e.g., nuts, garnish, gluten, soy sauce, honey)
- **Adapt** - offer additions, subtractions (can be made without X, Y or Z) or substitutions
- **Remember accessories** - vegan milk, bread and spreads; gluten-free bread and wraps; etc.

15.2 Insights from the industry

Aimee Louise McKinnon, UK—14 years in executive, head and sous chef roles

Vegans are easy. If I know I've got a table of veggies and vegans coming in, I'll make some aquafaba mayo and some special dessert treats for them. I make carrot bacon for BLTs, etc. It's important to recognise that everyone is a customer, valued, regardless of their lifestyle choice, diet or allergies. But it works both ways. In my eyes, customers should be a little more patient and understanding that we can't magic food out of thin air.

Tip

Invite and encourage customers with dietary preferences to book ahead of time and give advance notice. Doing so welcomes them and demonstrates options are available, and it ensures a better experience for both your business and the customers.

Jacqui McPeake, UK—owner of JACS Ltd. (food allergen and catering specialist), formerly head of catering at a large university

It's about making that food suitable for most people. For example, using a gravy or stock without the common allergens (like celery), so it is suitable for most diets. Some of the main suppliers now have taken out all those allergens so it is suitable for all. Why make it difficult?

Why not make a dish that is suitable for many?

For example, the chefs in the kitchen were doing beef bourguignon. There were six orders that were gluten free. They cooked the meat, then they separated it into 2 containers.

I said, *"Why are you doing it twice?"*

"Well, this one has the proper gravy in and that one has gluten-free stock. It won't taste the same, will it, love?"

I said, *"It will!"*

Tip

Save time and money by preparing inclusive dishes.

Jackie Norman, New Zealand—author and owner of a PR business and vegan hospitality consultancy

Obviously being-gluten free I am biased, but a lot of vegans are also gluten-free, and it can be an enormous challenge to find a dish which is both vegan AND gluten-free. I would really encourage eating establishments to serve options which are not only vegan but also gluten-free from the start. That way you always have all bases covered!

Tip

Making a clean vegan option that's also gluten-free will allow you to serve even more dietary preferences. If you have a dedicated vegan fryer or grill, consider whether you can make that equipment dedicated gluten-free as well.

Claire Smith, UK—vegan entrepreneur and investor, co-founder of Beyond Animal
It's all about choice. I would like to see everything turned upside down. Instead of me going into a restaurant and seeing the default being an option with meat or chicken, I would like to see the vegan option as the default, set at price X. If you want to add meat, it can often be made separately and mixed in or put on top.

Tip

Start with a great inclusive base dish (at a base price) and allow add-ins and customizations. You can serve more people while also using a pricing structure that will be perceived as fair.

Dennis Wilson, Canada—founder and rapid sales growth expert at Small Business Dream (a marketing automation tool) and DeliveryBizConnect
I 100% agree. Change your regular menu so that you are using things you can make good vegan dishes from, but you don't have to carry extra inventory for it. You solve all your problems at once.

Tip

Mindset is the first step. When you centre the goal of inclusivity, you can find ways to offer great food, increase choice *and* reduce food waste.

Sonalie Figueiras, Hong Kong—founder and editor-in-chief of *Green Queen Media*

Plant-based food consumers are now savvier than ever, and they want healthier alternative foods. That means shorter ingredients labels, "cleaner" products, less fat and fewer additives. This trend will become increasingly important as shoppers become less forgiving of meat alternatives and allow newer players to carve out their niche on the shelves.

Tip

When you develop inclusive offerings, keep in mind what motivates many dietary preferences: ethics, health and sustainability concerns.

Coral Sirett, UK—Zest Health, food service consultancy for plant-based wellness and plant-based weight loss; nutrition coach

Think about how to make it a balanced meal. So many vegan options can be very high in fat or carbs and very low in protein. And it's not difficult to get a decent amount of protein into a meal. You've just got to know what you're doing with it.

It also can be very diverse and very culturally inclusive. Where do we get our inspiration? What sort of foods do we eat? What are their origins? Are they Mexican, African, Indian,

Cantonese, Mediterranean, Middle Eastern, Lebanese? I'm not talking about the food they necessarily eat now, but a lot of their traditional food would be naturally vegan.

Petros Constantinos Jaferis, US—executive chef at Frontier Management Senior Living Communities

"Are you familiar with Lebanese garlic sauce? It's simple. Four ingredients: garlic, lemon, olive oil, salt. You blitz the lemon and the garlic, add in your oil a little by little, afterwards the salt until it's at the level you want. It's going to be very thick like mayonnaise, but just light lemon & garlic.

The main challenge really is just…planning. I hammer into all of my people, "Proper preparation prevents poor performance." We know who we have. We know what they eat. How do we not only prepare set menus for them, but have a bit of spontaneity if they want something different or off-the-cuff?

I'm from a Greek background, like a lot of my chef friends. I have some Lebanese chef friends and Indian chef friends. And especially in North Africa, there's a lot more vegetarians there per capita. So, what we do is we just exchange ideas."

James Brooks, UK—founder of Team Brooks, social media marketing for food and beverage brands

"What you might lack in cheese you can make up in colour. Toppings to make it pop and stand out. I love the coconut-based cheeses as well. They are very melty and great for food styling."

Tip

Approach your inclusive offerings with the same level of thought given to the other items on your menu. Those with dietary preferences also want something substantial and filling, interesting and tasty. Remember: thoughtful and interesting doesn't have to mean complicated and costly.

166

Inclusive Is the New Exclusive

The possibilities and inspiration for inclusive options are limitless and can fit almost any business concept. There are also resources and support for every part of the process—you can find many of them in the links at the end of this book.

So much has changed within hospitality this past year. Because of the pandemic-driven shifts in the industry, there is both a need and an opportunity for businesses who can serve niche markets alongside their core customers. Serving inclusively is hard work, but it is both achievable and worth doing.

Wherever you are on the journey, I would love to help you plan your next steps.

Book Takeaways

- The Common Denominator: Everyone has to eat.
- The Network Effect: Provide excellent customer service and people will rave about it.
- Be aware of the Dunning-Kruger Effect and the Curse of Knowledge.
- The market for dietary preference is bigger than society perceives.
- The occurrence of allergies and food intolerances is rapidly increasing, as is the number of people following plant-based or vegan diets.
- Not everyone fits into a box or follows a standard definition's "rules." The plant-based continuum is made up of continuums.
- Start with mindset: Are you in or are you out?
- Inclusivity is excellent customer service built on heightened food safety standards.
- Always be honest. Communication is key.
- A clean vegan option solves many problems. If you please a vegan, you please a lot of other people.

Bonus content includes:

Bonus Chapter
bonuschapter.heatherlandex.com

Free Resources
freeresources.heatherlandex.com

You can download your own Teal App PDF colour poster at
teal.heatherlandex.com

If you want me to audit your customer journey and/or optimise
your marketing and communication (whilst improving food
safety), get in touch at **Heather@heatherlandex.com.**

See also **Author Recommended Resources** at the back of the book.

Dear Reader,

Thank you for taking the time to read my book. Your feedback is very welcome. Reach out to me at heather@heatherlandex.com.
I am also working toward being more inclusive and understanding other perspectives. It is an endless learning journey.
I truly hope that you leave this book feeling thoughtful and inspired. I hope I have helped you see opportunity to improve your own service and how to **earn more, risk less.**
Maybe you're thinking I may be on to something—I certainly hope so. Have I sparked any creative ideas or inspired action? Have I given you enough to move you forward with the idea of inclusivity? I'm interested in helping you on your journey.
Becoming inclusive starts with putting yourself in your customers' shoes. It's beyond the ideas in this book, beyond categories like vegan or halal or gluten-free or nut-free.
It is about seeing people as individuals and considering customer needs.

I hope to see you in my *The Ultimate Starter* course. Connect with me on LinkedIn and tell me about your wonderful success out in the world.
All the best,

Heather

P.S. Join me to further develop your competitive edge in my free online course and forum at ultimatestarter.heatherlandex.com

Acknowledgements

First and foremost, I want to thank my husband, Alex. Without him, I would have never taken on such a big project during lockdown. I would never have finished, never have dared move away from the standard work of a food safety auditor. He has my back and has covered all my other priorities whilst I was writing. He is the original contributor to this book; without meeting him, I'd probably never have become vegetarian in the first place. Thank you for making life easier for me.

Writing this book has been an adventure full of emotional highs and lows, professional development and self-discovery. Alex has had to deal with a lot: childcare, an often absent or distracted wife and mother, edits and more edits, cuts and rewrites, interviews and other meetings, trainings and coaching.

He has fulfilled many roles. Alex is the co-creator of ideas and infographics, and he has been the project manager and therapist keeping me calm while nudging me out of my comfort zone into the online world of marketing and communication. I would not be the person I am today without his support and encouragement.

This process has changed me, challenged me and made me appreciate my lovely husband, home, children and lifestyle, despite the pandemic disabling the industry I love and keeping me—like many others—away from close family, friends and my homeland.

Thank you, Alex, for allowing me to be me and release this book into the world. You are an absolute sweetheart and my soulmate.

Next: Inger Nordin—my fellow author, accountability buddy, business and life coach, and dear friend. It has been a joy to share the author's journey with you. You kept me on track with my book, interviews and ideas, but also with my well-being. I have you to thank for getting me through to publishing with my marriage and sanity intact. You've been there for me (sometimes very late-night!), always extraordinary, loving and kind. Best of luck with your upcoming book *The Power of You*[2]. (ingernordin.com)

To Millie Hall, Alison Quinn, Cindy Willcocks and Alice Jennings: thank you for being my buddies and encouraging me the entire way. I'm happy to know you. Your feedback, love and support has been invaluable. Millie, thank you for showing me the way to veganism. It has enriched my life and my health, and it's helped me find my purpose. Ali, thank you for your VA services (*AQVA*). Cindy, thank you for guiding me through how to self-publish a book like you (*Draw a Heart Around It*). Alice, thank you for your allergy support and insight from the very beginning, even before the book was conceived. And many thanks to all of you for sticking with my book in its various drafts.

Muhammad Asif, thank you for being the first to believe in me and my book, giving your time to chat, to MCA for sponsoring the book, and for your business insights and industry expertise. You are remarkable.

Mitali Deypurkaystha, thank you for your tips and advice in the self-publishing process.

The last few years have been a time of massive personal and professional growth in my life, and I have several mentors to thank for "kicking me in the butt" and forcing me out of my comfort zone to follow my dreams despite the risk of failing. Korie Minkus at Industry Rockstar, Gerry Robert and Leesa Landry at Blackcard Books, and Silke Egholm Sales Coach: your coaching and mentorship helped me find my way. I also would like to thank the Mindvalley community for helping me to stay sane through the first lockdown. Thank you to Calvin Correli, founder and CEO of Simplero, for teaching me that mindset is everything. Your collective expertise inspired this book in many profound ways.

Once more, I would like to thank all the contributors and beta readers of this book for deepening my knowledge by giving me your time, expertise and patience throughout this process. It is a joy to know you. Thank you for being open to this conversation around inclusivity, no matter what you eat. To David McGee and Jordi Casamitjana in particular: thank you for your great efforts and dedication to supporting me through the challenging editing process. I am forever grateful to my wonderful fellow vegans. You are both amazing.

Thanks to Stuart Ewen, Jono Jenkins and James Lipscombe for contributing the case studies in this book and granting me permission to talk about inclusivity in context. Thank you to the anonymous contributors in the book for your contributions and attempting to clear your quotes with your respective companies. Your authentic individual opinions and expert advice remain. Your time and encouragement are valuable.

And thank you, dear readers, for trusting me with your time and attention. I hope this book has the same degree of positive impact in your life that it's had in mine.

Author Tributes

ETHICAL VEGAN

A personal and political journey to change the world

Jordi casamitjana

ISBN 978-1912836581

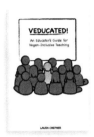

LETTERS TO JOSEP

An introduction to judaism

Daniella Levy

ISBN 978-9659254002

VEDUCATED!

An Educator's Guide for Vegan-Inclusive Teaching

Laura Chepner

ISBN 978-1940184623

DRAW A HEART AROUND IT

A revolutionary mental health treatment for individuals and companies

Cindy Willcocks

ISBN 978-1916074507

BE...

From passion and purpose to product and prosperity

Ashley Black with Korie Minkus and Lisa Vrancken

ISBN 978-1642937886

Everyday Vegan: EASY AND DELICIOUS

Vegan recipes for busy people

Jackie Norman and Gareth Scurr

ISBN 978-1760791414

CLEAN DISHES CLEAR PROFITS

How to maximise profits through your commercial dishwashing systems.

Richard Hose

ISBN 978-1781334508

A COMPLETE GUIDE TO CREATING TASTY SPACES

Designing, Planning & Building Post COVID-19 Food Facilities

Felicia Lisa Middleton

ISBN 978-1080002122

Contributors

Many individuals contributed to the development of this book with their time, expertise and experiences. Although not everyone who generously agreed to speak with me is quoted in these pages, the insights of the following people made this book better in ways both big and small.

Aimee Louise McKinnon - *Head Chef*	*UK*
Alex Landex – *Former Conference Organiser, Specialist Consultant*	*Denmark*
Alice Jenning – *Office Manager*	*Denmark*
Araceli Santos Serrano – *Manager Impronta*	*Denmark*
Birte Brorson –*Self-employed Teacher & Consultant in Commercial Kitchens*	*Denmark*
Carissa Kranz – *Founding Attorney / CEO of BeVeg International (global vegan certification firm)*	*US*
Caron Pollard – *Allergy Mum & Digital Marketing Expert, Co-Founder at Teal App*	*UK*
Casper Gorniok – *MBA CMktr, Author & Marketing Manager*	*UK*
Catherine Sharman – *Apres Food Co*	*UK*
Cesare Varallo – *Food Lawyer*	*Italy*
Charlotte-Annabel Jago – *Project Manager & Health Coach*	*Switzerland*
Chris Jenner - *Insight Manager at Winterbotham Darby & Co*	*UK*
Christian Christensen – *CEO at Dryk*	*Denmark*
Cindy Willcocks – *Founder of Arterne CIC & the L.O.V.E Leadership Academy*	*UK*
Claire Smith – *Vegan Entrepreneur, Co-Founder Beyond Animal & Vegan Investor*	*UK*
Claire Williams - *Senior Programme Manager*	*UK*
Clive Sheppard – *Founder of Zero Procure*	*UK*
Coral Sirett - *Zest Health Food Service Consultancy for Plant-Based Wellness & Plant Based Weight-loss & Nutrition Coach*	*UK*
Daniella Levy - *Author of Letters to Josep: An Introduction to Judaism*	*Israel*
Dave Bass - *Vegetarian Friend*	*UK*
David Pannel & Lisa Fox – *Co-founders at Vegan Business Tribe*	*UK*
Dennis Wilson – *Founder & Rapid Sales Growth Expert at Small Business Dream Marketing Automation Tool & DeliveryBizConnect*	*Canada*
David McGee - *Director at Hayfields Consultancy Ltd*	*UK*
Elena Boriani, PhD – *Consultant at EB Consultant*	*Denmark*
Felicia Middleton – *Author, Food Service Design Consultant, Foodie Builder at Urban Aesthetics*	*US*

Fran Collison – *Safety Director, UK* UK

George Robertson - *CEO at Emist* US

Hartej Kahai - *Your Vegan Marketer, Digital Marketer, Customer acquisition, Paid Search & Off-Page SEO Consultant* Canada

Hélène Moulin - *Directeur Fondateur at Chefs en Cuisine* Switzerland

Henrik Saxe - *Director of Mindful FOOD Solutions, formerly Associate Professor at DTU, KU and SDU Universities* Denmark

Jackie Norman - *Author, Owner - PR business & Vegan Hospitality Consultant* New Zealand

Jacqui McPeake – *Owner of JACS Ltd (Food Allergen and Catering Specialist)* UK

James Brooks – *Founder Team Brooks social media marketers* UK

James Lipscombe - *CEO & Owner of The Chesterford Group* UK

Jono Jenkins - *Lounge Head of Food* UK

Jordi Casamitjana - *Author of Ethical Vegan* UK

José Luis Cabañero - *Founder & CEO at Eatable Adventures - Global Food Innovation Hub* Spain

Julian Edwards – *CEO at Allergen Accreditation* UK

Kayleigh Nicolaou – *Kakadu Creative - A Different Design Agency* UK

Kevin Newall – *Founder of Humane Wildlife Solutions* UK

Khalid Latif – *Chaplin at New York University, Director of NYUs Islamic Centre, Owner of Honest Chops & Burgers by Honest Chops Restaurant.* US

Laura Chepner – *Vegan Inclusion Education Specialist, Owner at Primary Veducation & Author of An Educator's Guide for Vegan-Inclusive Teaching* UK

Laura San Segundo - *Group Marketing & Event Director at PRYSM Food & Drink Ltd.* UK

Loui Blake - *Plant-based Investor, Restaurant Entrepreneur & Speaker* UK

Maria Quereda - *Country Director for MCA Spain & Hospitality Operations Specialist* Spain

Mark McCulloch – *CEO and Founder of Brand & Market Consultancy - Supersonic Inc* UK

Mark Morgan-Huntley - *Chef, Founder & Director of Allergen Checker Ltd., (software to help chefs manage allergens allergenchecker.co.uk)* UK

Mette Johannsen – *Office Manager at The Vegetarian Society of Denmark, The Green Heart & V-Label* Denmark

Michael Lykke - *Founder of Okayfood software to assist dietary requirement information management.* Denmark

Millie Hall - *Approved Mental Health Professional (AMHP) & Ethical Vegan* UK

Muhammad Asif – *CEO at Main Course Associates* UK

175

Nicola Phillips - *Business Development Manager at Hospitality Action*   UK

Nivi Jaswal – *Plant Based Investor, Non-Profit Entrepreneur & Research Innovator*   US

Paul Adeniji - *Chef Director at Red Banana*   UK

Petros Constantinos Jaferis - *Executive Chef at Frontier Management.*   US

Rachel Baird Alahmad - *ESL Teacher & Globe Trotter*   US

Richard Ebbs – *Director of Commercial & Marketing at Synergy Grill*   UK

Richard Hose - *Author of Clean Dishes Clear Profits*   UK

Robert Bradley – *Director at Solar Compliance Ltd. & Learnsafe*   UK

Rookie Davies – *Owner of Wombie's Kitchen*   UK

Saadia Faruqi - *Author & Interfaith Activist*   US

Santi Aliaga - *CEO Zyrcular Foods*   Spain

Sonalie Figueiras - *Founder & Editor-in-Chief of Green Queen Media*   Hong Kong

Stuart Ewen - *Co-Founder of Mindset Associates*   UK

Surinder Thomas - *Co-Founder 2IG Ltd. trading as Hiya – Gluten Free, Vegan Snack Bars*   UK

Tarryn Gorre - *CEO & Co-founder of Kafoodle*   UK

Veronica Mauri - *Chef & Healthy Living Expert*   US

Victoria Williams - *Founder & CEO of terptree*   UK

Bibliography

AAAAI - American Academy of Allergy Asthma and Immunology. Allergy Definition. Available at: https://www.aaaai.org/conditions-and-treatments/conditions-dictionary/allergy

AAAAI - American Academy of Allergy Asthma and Immunology, Alpha-gal and Red Meat Allergy. Available at https://www.aaaai.org/conditions-and-treatments/library/allergy-library/alpha-gal

Agriculture and Horticulture Development Board, 2020 Consumer Insight November 2020. Available at: https://projectblue.blob.core.windows.net/media/Default/Consumer%20and%20Retail%20Insight%20Images/November%202020/UnconsciousReducers3904_WEB.pdf

Al-Mazeedi, Hani M., 2013, Joe M. Regenstein, and Mian Nadeem Riaz The Issue of Undeclared Ingredients in Halal and Kosher Food Production: A Focus on Processing. Comprehensive Reviews in Food Science and Food SafetyrVol.12, Institute of Food Technologists. Available at: https://www.researchgate.net/publication/259685903_The_Issue_of_Undeclared_Ingredients_in_Halal_and_Kosher_Food_Production_A_Focus_on_Processing_Aids

AllergyUK. Allergy Prevalence. Useful Facts and Figures. Available at: https://www.allergyuk.org/assets/000/001/369/Stats_for_Website_original.pdf?1505209830

Anaphylaxis UK , Companies that produce food for vegans are facing an interesting allergy-related dilemma. https://www.anaphylaxis.org.uk/2019/01/29/companies-that-produce-food-for-vegans-are-facing-an-interesting-allergy-related-dilemma/

Anaphylaxis UK Food Intolerance. Available at: https://www.anaphylaxis.org.uk/knowledgebase/food-intolerance/

BBC 20 November 2019 "Vegan sues Burger King for cooking Impossible Whopper on meat grill" Available at https://www.bbc.com/news/world-us-canada-50486664

Beyond Celiac, 2021. Non-celiac gluten sensitivity. Available at: https://www.beyondceliac.org/celiac-disease/non-celiac-gluten-sensitivity/

BeVeg Certification. Vegan Business and Restaurant Certification. https://www.beveg.com/vegan-business-and-restaurant-certification/

Brand Reputation Compliance Global Standards (BRCGS), Issue 1 Plant-Based Global Standards January 2020. Available at: https://1ilncn2p-tox93ih9e41q8but-wpengine.netdna-ssl.com/uk/wp-content/uploads/

sites/24/2020/11/Plant-Based-1-Standard-Locked-PDF.pdf

British Dietetic Association, 2021, Food Allergy and Food Intolerance: Food Fact Sheet. Available at: https://www.bda.uk.com/resource/food-allergy-food-intolerance.html

Coeliac UK, Coeliac Disease. Available at https://www.coeliac.org.uk/information-and-support/coeliac-disease/

Diabetic UK, 2021. Veganism and Diabetes. Available at: https://www.diabetes.org.uk/guide-to-diabetes/enjoy-food/eating-with-diabetes/veganism-and-diabetes

Dunning & Kruger, 1999 Unskilled and unaware of it: how difficulties in recognizing one's own incompetence lead to inflated self-assessments. Journal of personality and social psychology. Available at https://pubmed.ncbi.nlm.nih.gov/10626367/

European Commission. Food information to consumers – legislation. Available at: https://ec.europa.eu/food/safety/labelling_nutrition/labelling_legislation/fair-information-practices_en

European Vegetarian Union. 2018 Food Information Regulation: Which Food is Suitable for Vegans and Vegetarians? Available at: https://www.euroveg.eu/public-affairs/food-information-regulation/

FAO, Food and Agriculture Organisation of the United Nations), Solutions for reducing food loss and ensuring sustainable fishing livelihoods Available at: http://www.fao.org/in-action/bycatch-solutions-latin-america-caribbean/en/

FAO/WHO (Food and Agriculture Organisation of the United Nations / World Health Organisation), What is Codex Alimentarius? Available at: http://www.fao.org/fao-who-codexalimentarius/about-codex/en/#c453333

FAO/WHO (Food and Agriculture Organisation of the United Nations / World Health Organisation). General Guidelines for Use of the Term "Halal". Available at: http://www.fao.org/3/Y2770E/y2770e08.htm

Finder UK Jan 2021 UK diet trends 2021, 13 million Brits will be meat-free by the end of the year. Available at: https://www.finder.com/uk/uk-diet-trends

Foedevarestyrelsen (Danish Veterinary and Food Administration). Risikoanalyse for små engrosvirksomheder. Available at: https://www.foedevarestyrelsen.dk/Selvbetjening/Guides/Sider/Risikoanalyse-for-smaa-engrosvirksomheder.aspx

Food Allergy Research and Education (FARE), Food Allergy & Anaphylaxis, Available at: https://www.foodallergyawareness.org/food-allergy-and-anaphylaxis/food-allergy-basics/food-allergy-basics/

178

Food and Drink Federation 2020, FDF Guidance on 'Allergen'-Free and Vegan Claims. Available at https://www.fdf.org.uk/fdf/resources/publications/guidance/allegen-free-and-vegan-claims-guidance/

Food and Drug Administration (FDA) US, November 2020, Draft Guidance for Industry: Voluntary Disclosure of Sesame As An Allergen. Available at https://www.fda.gov/regulatory-information/search-fda-guidance-documents/draft-guidance-industry-voluntary-disclosure-sesame-allergen

Food Standards Agency, **FSA** UK 2016, J.Barrett. The preferences of those with food allergies and/or intolerances when eating out (FS305013) FINAL REPORT. Available at https://www.food.gov.uk/sites/default/files/media/document/fs305013-final-report.pdf

Food Standards Agency, FSA,UK Jan 2020 Foodborne Disease Estimates for the United Kingdom in 2018. Available at https://www.food.gov.uk/sites/default/files/media/document/foodborne-disease-estimates-for-the-united-kingdom-in-2018_0.pdf

Food Standards Agency, FSA, UK 2020 Nov, Allergen Guidance for Food Businesses. Available at https://www.food.gov.uk/business-guidance/allergen-guidance-for-food-businesses

Food Standards Agency, **FSA**, UK Food Allergen Labelling and Information Requirements: Technical Guidance – June 2020, https://www.food.gov.uk/sites/default/files/media/document/fsa-food-allergen-labelling-and-information-requirements-technical-guidance_0.pdf

Food Standards Agency, **FSA**, UK. Young people and food allergies and intolerances. Available at https://www.food.gov.uk/research/food-allergy-and-intolerance-research/young-people-and-food-allergies-and-intolerances

Food Standards Agency, **FSA**, UK. Safer food, better business (SFBB). Available at: https://www.food.gov.uk/business-guidance/safer-food-better-business-sfbb

Food Standards Agency, **FSA**, UK Food Hygiene Rating Scheme. Available at: https://www.food.gov.uk/safety-hygiene/food-hygiene-rating-scheme

Food Standards Agency, **FSA**, UK Key Regulations. Available at: https://www.food.gov.uk/about-us/key-regulations

Gerry Robert 2013, Multiply Your Business. Lifesuccess Publishing, ISBN: 978-1-77204-838-4

Grandview Research Inc, Feb 2020 "Gluten-Free Products Market Size, Share & Trends Analysis Report By Product (Bakery Products, Dairy/Dairy Alternatives), By Distribution Channel (Grocery Stores, Mass Merchandiser), By Region, And

Segment Forecasts, 2020 – 2027" Available at https://www.grandviewresearch.com/industry-analysis/gluten-free-products-market.

Heine et al,2017. Lactose intolerance and gastrointestinal cow's milk allergy in infants and children – common misconceptions revisited. World Allergy Organization Journal. Available at: https://waojournal.biomedcentral.com/articles/10.1186/s40413-017-0173-0

Hong Kong's Centre for Food Safety, The Government of Hong Kong Special Administrative Region. Food Legislation / Guidelines. Available at https://www.cfs.gov.hk/english/food_leg/food_leg_lgfa.html

Jordi Casamitjana, 2021, Ethical Vegan: A Personal and Political Journey to Change the World. September Publishing (UK) ISBN: 978-1912836581

KLBD Kosher Certification, 2021, What is Kosher? Available at: https://www.klbdkosher.org/what-is-kosher-certified/

Michael Greger (MD) and Gene Stone, 2015. How Not To Die. Pan Books. ISBN: 978-1-5098-5250-5

Morten Munsten, 2019, "I'm Afraid Debbie From Marketing Has Left for the Day - How to Use Behavioural Design to Create Change in the Real World", Gyldendal, ISBN: 978-8702275834

NHS, UK (National Health Service), Overview, Lactose intolerance. Available at https://www.nhs.uk/conditions/lactose-intolerance/

Statista 2018, Dietary restrictions in the United Kingdom (UK) 2018, Available at: https://www.statista.com/statistics/694497/dietary-restrictions-in-the-united-kingdom-uk/

The Guardian 3 October 2018, Pret a Manger to bring in full labelling after teenager's death. Available at https://www.theguardian.com/uk-news/2018/oct/03/pret-a-manger-to-bring-in-full-labelling-teenagers-death-natasha-ednan-laperouse

The Vegan Society, Allergen Labelling. Available at: https://www.vegansociety.com/resources/nutrition-and-health/allergen-labelling-0

The Vegan Society. Definition of Veganism. Available at: https://www.vegansociety.com/go-vegan/definition-veganism

The Vegan Society. Vegan Trademark Standards. Available at: https://www.vegansociety.com/vegan-trademark/vegan-trademark-standards

The Vegetarian Society, UK What is a vegetarian? Available at: https://vegsoc.org/info-hub/definition/

Uptodate *2020, Food intolerance and food allergy in adults: An overview,* Available at: https://www.uptodate.com/contents/food-intolerance-and-food-allergy-in-adults-an-overview

V-label, *Criteria of the V-Label: Regulations.* https://www.v-label.eu/regulations_text

Veganuary Campaign 2020. Veganuary 2020 Campaign In Review. Available at: https://veganuary.com/wp-content/uploads/2020/10/Veganuary-EndOfCampaignReport.pdf

W.Loh and M.Tang, Sept 2018 "Epidemiology of Food Allergy in the Global Context" in the International Journal of Environmental Research and Public Health. Available at https://www.ncbi.nlm.nih.gov/pmc/articles/PMC6163515

World Allergy Organisation 2017, Food Allergy. Available at: https://www.worldallergy.org/education-and-programs/education/allergic-disease-resource-center/professionals/food-allergy

World Population Review, 2021, Muslim Population by Country 2021, Available at: https://worldpopulationreview.com/country-rankings/muslim-population-by-country

World Population Review, 2021, Lactose Intolerance by Country 2021, Available at: https://worldpopulationreview.com/country-rankings/lactose-intolerance-by-country

Glossary

This is a simple, informal glossary provided to help you under-stand various concepts as they are discussed in the context of this book. Of course, many words can be interpreted to suit an individual or take on different meanings in other contexts. You are both welcome and encouraged to seek out additional clarifi-cations, explanations or details on any of these terms.

ACTIVIST a person who campaigns for political or social change. Synonyms – campaigner, advocate, demonstrator

ADULTERATION the action of making something poorer in quality by the ad-dition of another substance; the deliberate addition of something unwanted in food or knowingly failing to prevent contamination

"ALLEGEDIES" a term I coined for people who say they have an allergy when no such allergy has been diagnosed (alleged allergies)

ALLERGEN a substance that causes an allergic reaction; in the case of food allergy, usually a protein

ALLERGIST a medical practitioner specializing in the diagnosis and treatment of allergies

ALLERGY the atypical response of the body's immune system to normally harm-less substances such as pollens, foods, and dust mites

ALLERGY INCIDENT when someone has an allergic reaction, an occurrence

ANAPHYLACTIC adj., caused by anaphylaxis; e.g. anaphylactic shock

ANAPHYLAXIS an acute allergic reaction to an allergen (e.g. peanuts) to which the body has become hypersensitive

ANTIHISTAMINE a class of drugs commonly used to treat symptoms of allergies and conditions caused by too much histamine, a chemical created by your body's immune system.

APOLLO-VEGETARIAN vegetarian plus chicken

AUDITING conducting an inspection or check; in this context it refers to a third party auditor visiting a food business to check food safety or allergy management

AVERSION a strong dislike or revulsion caused by a sensitivity to smell, texture, or taste; may cause symptoms of physically illness but it is not related to allergies

BIODIVERSITY the variety of plant and animal life in the world or in a par-ticular habitat, a high level of which is usually considered to be important and desirable.

BRAND image, design and reputation

BRAND PROTECTION protection of image and reputation; in this context we are talking about protecting the name of the company from bad PR, media, litigation or customer complaints

CARNIVORE an animal that feeds on other animals

CARCINOGENIC adj. for something believed to cause cancer

CHOLESTEROL Cholesterol is a type of fat found in your blood. Your body can make all the cholesterol it needs. Cholesterol is only found in foods that come from animals; there is no cholesterol in foods that come from plants. People with high cholesterol are prone to heart disease.

CLEAN VEGAN OPTION a vegan product or dish without "may contain" animal products disclaimer; it is therefore allergy-friendly/free-from animal product allergens (fish, milk, egg, shellfish, and any animal products to which people may be allergic)

CODEX ALIMENTARIUS international food standards from the FAO/WHO to assist in fair trade

COELIAC DISEASE (Celiac Disease in US English) a condition where someone's immune system attacks their own tissues when they eat gluten, damaging the gut (small intestine) so the person cannot take in nutrients

COLITIS a long-term condition where the colon and rectum become inflamed; thought to be an autoimmune disease

COMMON DENOMINATOR a feature shared by all members of a group; in this context, what everyone can eat

COMPLIANCE the name for the act or process of meeting rules, standards or legal requirements

COMPLIANT the status of meeting rules, standards or legal requirements

CONTAMINATION stuff in food we don't want in food; in this context, allergens or animal products, but may also refer to bacteria in the food service industry

CRITICAL CONTROL POINTS the points in the process of making food which are extremely important for safety; e.g., cooking food to the correct/a standard temperature

CRITICAL THINKING the objective analysis and evaluation of an issue in order to form a judgement

CROHN'S DISEASE a type of inflammatory bowel disease (IBD) causing inflammation of your digestive tract, which can lead to abdominal pain, severe diarrhoea, fatigue, weight loss and malnutrition

CROSS CONTACT a technical way to describe unintentional transfer of allergens from one substance or object to another (often called cross-contamination)

CROSS-CONTAMINATION the unintentional transfer of bacteria or microorganisms from one substance or object to another, with harmful effect (sometimes used to describe the unintentional transfer of allergens)

CRUSTACEA invertebrates with a hard exoskeleton (a shell), a symmetrical segmented body and an open circulatory system (e.g., crab, lobster, shrimp, barnacles)

CUE anything that excites to action; stimulus, a hint, guiding suggestion

CUSTOMER-CENTRIC an approach to doing business that focuses on providing a positive customer experience both at the point of sale and after the sale in order to drive profit and gain a competitive advantage

DEMOGRAPHICS statistical data relating to the population and particular groups within it (age, income, etc.)

DIABETES a chronic metabolic disease characterized by high blood sugar, which leads over time to serious damage to the heart, blood vessels, eyes, kidneys and nerves

DIETARY PREFERENCE in this context, a specialized diet or atypical way of eating that often leads to the individual being excluded from eating out (of the home)

DISABILITY a physical or mental condition that limits a person's movements, senses or activities

DISCLAIMER a statement that denies something, especially responsibility or liability

DIVERSITY variety; the inclusion or involvement of people from a range of different social and ethnic backgrounds and of different genders, sexual orientations, etc.

DUE DILIGENCE DEFENCE A legal defence demonstrating that you were not negligent and you followed the law in a case of, e.g., food poisoning. The documents and evidence you produced in your FSMS/HACCP show you took all reasonably practicable steps to reduce risk.

EDUTAINMENT an informal, entertaining style of education

ENFORCEMENT ACTION Action taken to force compliance with a law or requirement, such as food law; may include formal letters, notices regarding fines, forced improvements, closure, seizing of food or equipment, or criminal prosecutions

ENVIRONMENTAL HEALTH the branch of public health concerned with monitoring or mitigating those factors in the environment that affect human health and disease (such as the home and work environments, air, water and land pollution, food, control of infectious diseases)

ENVIRONMENTAL HEALTH PRACTITIONER also known as Environmental Health Officers or Public Health Officers; officials who are qualified and experienced in compliance or law enforcement to protect the public's health; often specialised in food safety, health and safety, environmental protection and pollution control or housing or various other functions on behalf of the government or in the private sector

ENZYME a substance produced by a living organism which acts as a catalyst to bring about a specific biochemical reaction; e.g., rennet, which is taken from calves' stomachs to curdle milk to make cheese and is usually a byproduct of slaughter

EQUALITY ACT 2010 UK UK legislation protecting people from discrimination in the workplace and in wider society; replaced previous anti-discrimination laws with a single act, making the law easier to understand and strengthening protection in some situations

ETHICAL VEGAN someone who not only follows a vegan diet but extends the philosophy into other areas of their lives, opposing the use of animals for any purpose

FLEXITARIAN definitions vary, but most commonly, a person who has a primarily vegetarian diet but occasionally eats meat or fish

FOOD HYGIENE RATING SCHEME (UK) rating scheme that reflects the standards of food hygiene found on the date of the inspection by the local authority; the rating is publicly accessible and in Wales and N. Ireland must be displayed at the business

FOOD SAFETY AUDITOR a qualified person who inspects food businesses processes or food handling practices to uphold legal or commercial food safety standards; may work for the government or private companies

FOOD SAFETY CULTURE the food safety attitudes, values and beliefs shared by staff within a food business; behaviours that determine the robustness of the food safety management system

FOOD SAFETY MANAGEMENT SYSTEM An approach to handling food safety that looks at each step of the journey food takes from delivery to being served to the customer. It assesses risks and hazards within, e.g., a kitchen and tries to control and reduce risk of injury or harm to customers by checking temperatures, times, labels and traceability to make sure everything is as it should be. It usually also takes into account system-supporting policies such as staff sickness, pest control or cleaning.

FOOD SAFETY STANDARDS The agreed set of rules, practices, processes, policies an individual food business must follow. Countries have their own legal food safety standards, as does the EU, but companies, particularly large companies and franchises, have common standards for all sites and outlets which are above the legal standards. There are international standards which are agreed upon as a good practices to effectively protect consumers from food poisoning or other harm from food.

FOOD HYPERSENSITIVITY Food Allergy (involves the immune system)

FOOD SENSITIVITY Food Intolerance (sometimes involves the immune system)

FOOD STANDARDS AGENCY (FSA) agency responsible for food safety and food hygiene in England, Wales and Northern Ireland; works with local authorities to enforce food safety regulations and check standards are being met

FRANCHISE an authorization granted by a brand or company to an individual or group enabling them to carry out specified commercial activities; for example, permission to open a branded restaurant (e.g., McDonalds is the biggest restaurant franchise in the world)

FRANCHISEE an individual or company that holds a franchise for the sale of goods or the operation of a service

GLUTEN a protein found in wheat and other cereals

GLUTEN INTOLERANCE (SENSITIVITY) condition in which the body has difficulty digesting gluten; the individual experiences symptoms similar to those of coeliac disease, yet lacks the antibodies and intestinal damage seen in coeliac disease

HACCP Hazard Analysis Critical Control Point

HALAL Halal describes anything permissible or lawful under Islamic law, as defined in the Koran

HEALTH INEQUALITIES unfair and avoidable differences in health outcomes among different groups within a society

HISTAMINE a chemical produced by the immune system which causes inflammation (and itching)

IGE a specific immunoglobulin produced by the immune system (antibody)

IMMUNOCOMPROMISED having lower immunity than the populational average

IMMUNOLOGY study of the immune system

IMMUNOSUPPRESSANT a drug that suppresses the immune response of an individual

INCIDENCE the number of people who experience an event; in this context food poisoning or allergic reaction to food

INCLUSIVITY the practice or policy of including people who might otherwise be excluded or marginalized, such as minority groups

INTOLERANCE 1. unwillingness to accept views, beliefs, or behaviour that differ from one's own

2. an inability to eat a food or take a drug without adverse effects

IRRITABLE BOWELS SYNDROME (IBS) a common condition that affects the digestive system, causing symptoms like stomach cramps, bloating, diarrhoea and constipation; symptoms tend to come and go over time and can last for days, weeks or months at a time

KOSHER a term used to describe food that complies with the strict dietary standards of traditional Jewish law

LACTASE an enzyme that breaks down lactose (a sugar)

LACTOSE a sugar found in milk (cows, goats, sheep, humans, and many other mammals)

LACTOSE INTOLERANCE a common digestive problem where the body is unable to digest lactose, a type of sugar mainly found in milk and dairy products

LIABILITY the state of being legally responsible for something

LEGAL MINIMUM REQUIREMENTS according to the law, the requirements that food businesses must meet to prevent harm or injury to people

LITIGATION the process of taking legal action

LUPIN A legume (plant); lupin flour and seeds can be used in some types of bread, pastries and pasta

MEAT EATER my term for someone who eats more meat than recommended or than is typical

MICROORGANISMS bacteria, viruses, very small parasites; commonly known as germs

MINDSET the established set of attitudes held by someone

MISE EN PLACE (in a professional kitchen) the preparation of dishes and ingredients before the beginning of service

MOLLUSCS a large group of soft-bodied, legless invertebrate animals whose bodies are not divided into rings (but who may have tentacles); includes clams, mussels, oysters, scallops, octopi, squid, cuttlefish, nautili, snails and slugs

MOULD (MOLD IN US ENGLISH) a type of microscopic fungus that grows on or in food, producing toxins; can be carcinogenic

NIGHTSHADE VEGETABLES vegetables containing a specific alkaloid which can cause allergy; includes white potatoes, tomatoes, tomatillos, eggplants/aubergines, peppers, paprika

OMNIVORE an animal or person that eats a variety of food of both plant and animal origin

OVO-LACTO-VEGETARIAN vegetarian diet including eggs and milk

PESCATARIAN vegetarian diet plus fish (and other seafood)

PHILOSOPHICAL BELIEF a strong, genuine non-religious belief concerning an important aspect of human life and behaviour; includes things like humanism, secularism and atheism; protected in the UK under the Equality Act 2010

POLLEN FOOD SYNDROME a common medical condition, usually in people who suffer hay fever (allergic to pollen), which causes immediate allergic symptoms in the lips, mouth and throat after eating certain kinds of raw fruit or raw vegetables containing similar proteins to those in pollen

PREVALENCE the number of people with a disease; how common it is

PROBIOTIC live microorganisms believed to have health benefits when consumed

PROSECUTION conducting of legal proceedings against someone in respect of a criminal charge

REQUIREMENT a thing that is compulsory; a necessary condition (e.g., legal or contractual requirements)

RHINITIS inflammation of the mucous membrane of the nose, caused by a virus infection or by an allergic reaction

SHELLFISH aquatic animal with a shell, including molluscs and crustacea (e.g., lobster, crab, squid, octopi, oysters, snails, mussels, clams, scallops, barnacles, shrimp)

SOCIAL EXCLUSION exclusion from the social system and its rights and privileges, typically as a result of belonging to a minority social group

STATINS any of a group of drugs which act to reduce levels of cholesterol in the blood

SULPHITES a salt of sulphurous acid, naturally found in some foods, used as an additive to maintain food colour, extend shelf life and prevent the growth of fungi or bacteria; also used in food packaging

TYPICAL EATER my term for someone without the dietary preferences outlined in this book

UNIQUE SELLING POINT (USP) a feature or characteristic of a good or service that distinguishes it from others of a similar nature and makes it more appealing

VEGAN (ADJECTIVE) eating, using, or containing no animal products

VEGAN (NOUN) a person who does not consume (eat or use, increase demand for) animal products

VEGETARIAN (ADJECTIVE) relating to vegetarians or vegetarianism

VEGETARIAN (NOUN) a person who does not eat meat or fish, and sometimes other animal products, especially for moral, religious, or health reasons

VULNERABLE GROUPS people who may be immunocompromised (poor immunity) such as pregnant women, the elderly, children and infants, people with other health conditions

WHOLE FOOD PLANT BASED DIET a diet of foods from plants which have not been excessively processed

What do I know about inclusivity?
A lot, it turns out.

I have been vegan for a couple of years, vegetarian for a couple years before that, and flexitarian (mostly vegetarian plus chicken) for ten years before that...give or take. My diet went through radical short-term shifts whilst I was pregnant and again whilst I was breast-feeding. Back then, I gave up caffeine and tried to give up milk (unsuccessfully) because it gave me reflux. I have had numerous dietary needs and preferences in my life thus far. I know how it feels to be included and to be excluded.

In the preface I talk about my struggles with food allergies and an incident that triggered this inclusivity quest. My personal life has also affected my perspective in other ways: I am married to a lifelong vegetarian, and I have numerous friends and family members with different dietary preferences. I am also surrounded by (or have surrounded myself with!) experts who have helped me put other pieces of the inclusivity puzzle together.

My professional life has also given me unique insights. As an Environmental Health Practitioner working across eight countries, I have visited over 1000 food premises and audited hundreds of hotels and restaurants specifically for food safety and brand standards. Before that, I worked in three different countries as food and beverage staff in more than fifty food service businesses.

Because I embody the customer, auditor and employee perspectives and have learned from industry experts, I feel well placed to help both food businesses and their customers. Having lived in five countries as an adult, I can compare cultures.

What am I trying to say? I have a unique perspective, shaped by the places and experiences to which I have had access and what I have learned there. I can see the opportunities most cannot.

190

Author Recommended Resources

MCA

WE ARE THE LEADING HOSPITALITY, RESTAURANT & RETAIL INDUSTRY SPECIALISTS

Our aim is to put all our knowledge to work for each and every client and help drive their future success.

The Main Course Associates team is made up of industry insiders with over 150 years of combined experience. We understand the pressures involved in operating a business in hugely demanding sectors of Hospitality, Retail & Restaurants – and know how to overcome them.

We'll work in partnership with you to identify key areas of pressure, analyse how best to deal with them and then implement the changes to move you forwards. From strategy, finance to tactical planning we aim to add value throughout our relationship with you and bring our experience to bear on every project and every issue.

20 years of activity in the industry

4 key service lines

4 new business ventures directly funded

150+ yrs of combined experience

52 customers globally with a combined turnover of over £150m

Over £50m of funds raised to date for our customers

FINANCIAL MANAGEMENT

OPERATIONAL MANAGEMENT

F&B MANAGEMENT

STRATEGIC PLANNING

YOUR TRUSTED PARTNER FOR YOUR SUCCESS

SCAN FOR MCA TOP TIPS:

mcainternational.net

LONDON | MALAGA | MILAN | SAVONA | AMSTERDAM

A collaborative approach is at the heart of everything
we do at MCA. As your trusted partner we look to build lasting
relationships. Our culture supports our people who in turn
support our clients.

We have an international office & client base,
as a result we are able to bring a more considered,
bespoke approach and a global perspective.

Muhammad Asif | CEO | London
Founder of MCA International

With over 15 years of experience in the
industry, he has held many senior financial
& strategic roles. Asif is a Fellow Chartered
Qualified Accountant and a serial entrepreneur
who also invests in high growth firms.

Simple icons. Clear message

Our simple and clear food allergen and ingredient icons will help keep your customers informed, quickly and effectively.

 celery

crustaceans

 eggs

 fish

 milk

 molluscs

 cereals containing gluten

 mustard

 lupin

nuts

peanuts

 sesame seeds

 soya

 sulphur dioxide

 trace allergen

 ingredients

Ask yourself...

Do you feel safe when eating food you haven't prepared yourself?

Have you thought about offering customers the choices they want?

Do your customers trust you and what you are serving?

Do you have all the procedures in place to cover allergens?

Are you selling food that is pre-packed for direct sale? (PPDS)

Do you make wedding cakes, sell cakes at a fete for charities, make biscuits for sale?

Allergen Checker's unique software covers all your needs, from printed ingredient labels and menus all for £1 per day*

Sign up now for your **free 7-day trial!**

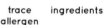

SCAN ME

*Yearly subscription is £360 incl. VAT and is required to print labels and menus

BeVeg VEGAN CERTIFICATION

Have a vegan product or service?
Make your claim *official*.

Apply now!

- Food/Beverages
- Pharmaceuticals
- Alcohol
- Textiles
- Cosmetics
- Restaurants/Lodging
- Manufacturing Facilities
- Private Label

Global trademark.

World's only ISO *accredited* vegan certification standard.

RECOGNIZED ON SIX CONTINENTS.

The allergy app designed to help you manage your allergies

TEAL

Allergy Tracker

Scan to download

DOWNLOAD YOUR POSTER
AT
WWW.TEAL.HEATHERLANDEX.COM

DIGITAL MARKETING EXPERT

 **your vegan marketer**

As an SEO and PPC Specialist, we completely understand your customers and the restaurant market. We offer consulting for improving your customer acquisition via digital marketing and create strategies to implement getting your website to the highest pages on search engines.

Improve search position rankings

Fully managed SEO service

Strategic customer aquisition plan

Unlimited keyword research

Outperform competitors

Free live tracking system

"303% increase in clicks in the last 90 days"

Use referral code: DIETSEO and get $300 off SEO

 hartej@yourveganmarketer.com

Ollie Hoile.
Catering Manager.
We've got you.

From Housekeepers to Concierge.
From Sous Chefs and Kitchen Porters
to Catering Managers like Ollie.
Whatever you do in hospitality,
isn't it good to know that someone's
got your back if life ever takes a
wrong turn?

If you need help call the
Hospitality Action Helpline
0808 802 0282
or visit our website
hospitalityaction.org.uk

Hospitality Action

HUMANE WILDLIFE SOLUTIONS

Revolutionising the Face of Pest Control

Isn't time you truly protected your business from wildlife

Our Services can protect your business and keep it safe for the future with its revolutionary proofing and preventative measures. This is followed by reports which can be used to comply with your environmental health commitments.

Contact us today to find out about how our proofing and preventative measures are helping food businesses all over Europe.

BENEFITS TO YOU

- Protects your reputation
- Protects your food stock
- Protects your staff health
- Protects your customers
- Protects your property
- Saves money
- No toxic poisons
- Rodent free

BOOK YOUR CONSULTATION TODAY

T: **0777 136 1226**
E: **info@humanewildlifesolutions.co.uk**
W: **www.humanewildlifesolutions.co.uk**

FOR ALL YOUR PLANT-BASED COACHING, CONSULTANCY & WELLNESS NEEDS

Food service consulting

Beat the competition with simple tweaks to your menus

Workplace wellness sessions

Increase productivity; save money; happy, healthy staff

Weight loss & nutrition coaching

Boost energy, feel more confident & in control of your eating

Coral Sirett

SCAN QR CODE FOR A FREE CONSULTATION

coral@zest-health.com

+44 7708 047580

zest-health.com

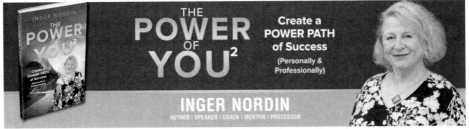

& it Has?...

"And it Has" is the Allergy & Ingredient App that helps Independent & Chain Businesses speak clearly & safely to the 35% of customers with dietary preferences.

We help your business celebrate your menu & share your allergen, ingredient & nutritional information with potential customers looking for safe places to eat in seconds by using our nearby list...

"And it Has":-

- Ensures great customer experience & increases confidence
- Supports staff to give clear, safe & factual information
- Reduces menu confusion & ensures efficient ordering
- Gets you ahead of legislation & reduces your liability
- Increases revenue opportunities & new customer reach
- PPDS Print on Demand Label Service linked to the app
- Lots of cool new tech on its way.

To find out more visit: **www.andithas.com**
Contact us at: **hello@andithas.com**

Scan to View and Filter our Digital Menu
Allergens - Full Ingredients - Nutritional Data

FREE App Download - **www.andithas.com**

Conbella
CREATIVE SOLUTIONS & PARTNERS

Around the world, people view the butterfly as representing

Endurance, Change, Hope & Life

From concept of your brand, packaging branding to sustainable eco-friendly packaging production.

- Inclusive Packaging and Label solutions.
- In-House Post Production, Artwork & Repro.
- Cost effective and speed of product to market.
- No MOQ's on Litho or Digital Print Runs.
- Large Format Digital Print.

Visit our web site for our vast array of services

Scan Our QR

Branding | Packaging & Label Design | Brand Guidelines | Artwork & Reprographics
Packaging Artwork Adaptation | Sustainable Packaging **&** Label Print Production
Large Format Digital Print | POS | POP UP Displays | FSDU | CDU | Pull UP Banners
Wall Graphics | Floor Graphics Window Graphics

your *packaging partner*   www.conbella.co.uk   *making tomorrow's possibilities* **today**

the NUTRIENT GAP
HEALTH FROM THE INSIDE OUT

Are your food labels accurate?
Are you up to date with the current legislation?

INGREDIENTS

- Compliancy on pre-packed goods for direct sale
- Natasha's Law
- Ingredient lists and allergy transparency
- Nutritional information
- Legal descriptors and nutritional claims
- New product development and reformulation
- Calorie information on menus
- Compliancy & allergen training

INFORMATION

Book a FREE 20-minute
Consultation with
The Nutrient Gap
Scan Our Barcode

GET YOUR BUSINESS HEALTHY FROM THE INSIDE OUT
e: georgina@thenutrientgap.com   t: 07814 735 489

NO ARTIFICIAL COLOURS OR FLAVOURINGS,
OR HYDROGENATED FAT USED IN THIS ADVERT